Grotz's
Antique Furniture Styles

Grotz's Antique Furniture Styles

GEORGE GROTZ

Doubleday

NEW YORK

1987

Library of Congress Cataloging-in-Publication Data

Grotz, George.
Grotz's Antique furniture styles.

1. Furniture—Styles. 2. Antiques. I. Title.
NK2235.G76   1987   749.2   86–32904
ISBN 0-385-19513-3

CONTENTS

STYLES IN TRANSITION

Now you can tell the style of a piece of antique furniture as accurately as any expert. And not only can you tell the basic style, but you can also point out the interesting variations in the pieces that were transitional from one style to the next. And believe me there are far more transitional pieces than "pure" ones.

After all, the cabinetmakers* of eighteenth-century London didn't one day all throw their hands up in the air and exclaim, "Well, that's enough of Queen Anne! Let's start making Chippendale!"

What actually happened was a gradual increase in popular taste for furniture that was more ornately decorated with acanthus leaves in the French style (the English have always had a recurring interest in what was going on over there in the sin pits of Paris), and this evolving style came to be called Chippendale.

Nor did the American furniture factories of the Victorian era suddenly stop making furniture in the Golden Oak style and start making Mission. In fact they made both styles at the same time—even on the same day in the same factory!

So each of the styles has its story and its place in history, because each style became popular in response to a public taste that was based on the spirit of the times. Thus we have the exuberance of the time of King Louis XV expressed in furniture that looks as though it might jump in the air.

On the other end of the scale, we have a Victorian philosopher's faith in the power of machinery expressed in the geometric precision of Eastlake decoration. And how about the serenity of the Queen Anne style, which reminds us of a swan gliding by on a quiet pond!

In all there are twenty-nine distinctive styles that we can choose from to express our own personalities or to create special moods in the various rooms we live in.

It's a feast. Come enjoy it!

GEORGE GROTZ

---

* "Cabinetmakers" refers to carpenters who made all types of furniture.

GLOSSARY

Some Terms Used in Describing Antique Furniture

apron   the piece connecting the legs beneath a top or main structure

bailles   loose handles of escutcheoned drawer pulls

bombe   swelled front like a pregnant woman

bonnet   curved top or hood on top of a highboy

boulle   brass sheet or tortoiseshell inlay into wood panels

bracket feet   chest or cabinet feet in shape of a corner brace

bun feet   turned ball foot flattened like a bun

burl   figure in veneers cut from the bulbous growths on trees

cabriol   double-curved leg from Italy used in the Queen Anne and Louis XV styles

caryatids   supporting columns in the shape of female figures; also used as legs

ditty box   a small box usually used by sailors to hold sewing implements and other necessities

ebonized   wood stained black and polished to look like ebony

étagère   open shelves used to display objects

fences   spindled-edge railings around furniture tops

finials   brass terminal on top of post or pediment

lyres   supports in chair backs shaped like Greek lyres

Marlborough   straight molded Chippendale leg

O.G./ogee   double curve molding

ormulu   ornate gilded brass applied furniture decoration. French

pediment   originally a triangular top on a highboy. Some are S-curved.

Pembroke   drop-leaf table with top wider than leaves

pillar and scroll   Roman decoration in those shapes on pediments

porringer   a bowl for eating porridge out of, or anything shaped like such a bowl

prie-dieu   prayer bench

scroll top   spiral-shaped ornamental carving

scrubbed top   one used as a kitchen or tavern table

settle   low bench with solid wood back and ends

sevres placques   hand-painted porcelain shapes used to decorate furniture
Spanish foot   rectangular ribbed foot with weak scroll
stretchers   runners between legs
tambour   sliding door made of thin reeds glued to canvas
turnings   wood posts and stretchers rounded in a lathe
vitrine   narrow display cabinet

Grotz's
Antique Furniture Styles

English Styles

The trouble with the use of the term Georgian

It so happens that during the golden century of furniture design—the eighteenth century—England was ruled by three King Georges in a row. And their reigns span the development (and overlapping) of the furniture styles we call Queen Anne, Chippendale, Adam, Hepplewhite, Sheraton, and Regency.

So when a piece of furniture is transitional between any two of these styles (and a great many pieces are), it makes a lot of sense to refer to it as being Early Georgian, Middle Georgian, or Late Georgian. It makes sense, that is, for people who are already familiar with the styles being blended, but it is of little help to people who are not yet familiar with all of the styles that come under the classification of Georgian.

So it seems useful to eschew the use of the term "Georgian" in a reference book of this kind, and instead to try, in every case, to point out the design details that come from each style in a given transitional piece. *However,* if you want to impress people with your superior knowledge of English history . . .

George I refers to the transitional pieces between Queen Anne and Chippendale. This is when carving first began to appear on the knees of Queen Anne legs and other decorative carving was moving toward the full-blown Chippendale style.

George II simply means the fully realized Chippendale style.

George III covers all of the furniture of the classical revival that was a result of the excavation of the Roman ruins at Pompeii and Heraculeum. That is Adam and Hepplewhite—and through the French-influenced Sheraton and Regency (the English version of Empire).

To complicate matters even more, in recent years another way of using the term Georgian has become popular. This is to use it only for Queen Anne and Chippendale and the very many pieces that are transitional between them. Then the following styles are called by their real names: Adam, Hepplewhite, Sheraton, and Regency.

Well, if all that is hard to swallow in one gulp, leafing through the following pages should clear it up for you. Then come back and read that paragraph again, and you will see what I mean.

P.S. Naturally, this nonsense about using the term Georgian also applies to English-style furniture made in the American colonies. All of the Georgian styles were made in New York City, Boston, and Philadelphia, which produced the especially well-known Philadelphia Chippendale, a more ornately carved and tastelessly fussy brand than the original. Primitive country versions of the Georgian styles were also made by country carpenters throughout New England and the middle Atlantic colonies up until the early years of statehood.

JACOBEAN, 1600–50

The first movable furniture emerges from the massive built-ins of the castles and monasteries of the Middle Ages.

The name "Jacob" is the Latin root of the English name "James." So the term "Jacobean" refers to the reign of King James I in England during the first half of the 1600s.

This was the beginning of the Renaissance in England, and during this time the first recognizable style of movable furniture emerged. Like the massive built-ins of the Middle Ages, it was mostly heavy chests that used the framed-panel method of construction. And the use of Gothic arches disappeared. The wood used was almost entirely oak, and the decoration mostly geometric—as opposed to the curves and floral decoration that were soon to follow.

This style was quite popular during the Roaring Twenties, when Americans first discovered that Europe had a history and William Randolph Hearst started bringing home castles full of it to impress Marion Davies, but its popularity has subsequently declined. During the twenties, many reproductions of Jacobean furniture were made. These can easily be detected by their lack of dry rot, which all of the original pieces have.

Much of Jacobean furniture is "important" because it was made for castles and great houses before the emergence of the middle class in eighteenth-century England. Here is an oak sideboard which has lost the braces that should run between the legs.

A walnut settle with a lift-top chest in the seat. All Jacobean furniture is made of walnut or oak, native English woods, and enthusiastically carved with leaves and floral designs. A front-hall chair with the inscription, "If tired and weary your feet should rest on me."

One of the best of the Jacobean pieces is the six-legged drop-leaf table.
Four legs in the center frame and two swing legs to hold up the leaves.
Strong, solid, and secure in heavy oak from the English forests. Bulb
turnings on legs work perfectly in this great piece.

Typical Jacobean oak dresser features geometric designs on drawer
fronts and tear-drop pulls, features which appeared at the end of the
period and reached into the following William and Mary style.

A useful small Jacobean chest of nice proportions and geometric drawer fronts. Baille or loop handle with simple escutcheon or back plate came into use at this time—to be developed in Queen Anne and Chippendale styles.

A *perfect* example of the Jacobean style in a piece that isn't too big for modern usage of furniture. The turned bun feet, the simple bulbous carving strips, the geometric doors, the tear-drop pulls with their little round escutcheons—it's all there.

Lift-top blanket chest. In the late 1600s and into the early 1700s, the Jacobean style appeared in the American colonies of New England, where it was called American Jacobean, or Pilgrim, style. It differed from the European Jacobean style in that here, arches and split-spindle turnings were applied as decoration.

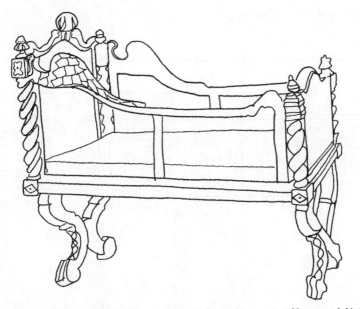

The elaborate carving of this cane and walnut cradle establish it as a Victorian reproduction in the Jacobean style. Many thousands of these cradles were made in England during the Victorian era. They are still popular and are probably still being made today.

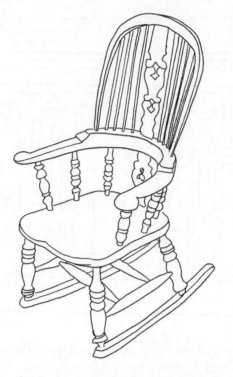

Broad-arm chair of oak that somebody had made into a rocker; it may be old enough to call Jacobean, though such chairs are commonly reproductions. An ancestor of the American Windsor chair.

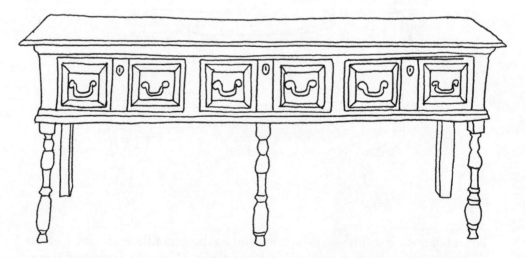

This six-legged Jacobean sideboard, server, or buffet is almost three feet high and nine feet long; it fits in nicely in most castles.

WILLIAM AND MARY, 1690–1710

The style of the trumpet leg that endured from the 1600s to the Roaring Twenties

It's a long story about how a Dutch king and his queen got to rule England for thirteen years at the end of the 1600s, but it did do wonders for the furniture business. William and Mary brought with them all sorts of new ideas in furniture design that were so interesting that they were still being reproduced in Grand Rapids in the 1920s and 1930s.

The most noticeable of these design ideas were the trumpet leg (like a trumpet upside-down), the curved stretchers and the Spanish foot. But there was also a lot of fancy decoration on the surfaces of these pieces. Some were Japanned (a process in which black lacquer is applied and brought to a mirror-smooth finish by French-polishing it with an oily pad) and had oriental sketches painted on them.

Also unique to the period is an incredibly fine and lacey marquetry called "seaweed." Marquetry means one veneer inlaid into another and both glued to a solid wood surface. Walnut was the wood used for practically all William and Mary furniture.

As to the availability, there are precious few authentic pieces around that are not in museums or the homes of California billionaires. But many reproductions of this style were made in Victorian England which are hard to tell from the originals—due to British craftsmanship and all that. It takes a careful examination of the interior cabinet to tell the difference.

Then, of course, there are the Grand Rapids reproductions, but these were all painted a dull yellowish-green for reasons unknown. And stripping the green paint off reveals that they are made of blocked pieces of poplar instead of solid boards of walnut.

The great bun feet are the most distinctively William and Mary design feature on this desk, but it also has burl walnut veneer on the drawer fronts. The drawer pulls are transitional into Queen Anne.

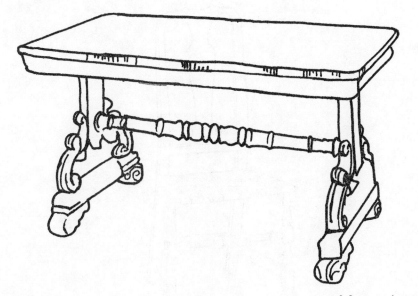

A walnut library table with burl veneer on the top. Many pieces of William and Mary are not that easy to identify. But the double-curve leg braces and Spanish feet in this piece are definitely of the style.

This slant-front desk contains all of the design features of William and Mary: trumpet legs, bun feet, curved stretchers, tear-drop drawer pulls, and satinwood inlay on dark walnut wood.

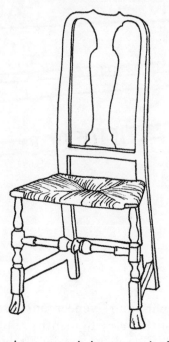

A clearly transitional piece containing a typical Queen Anne splat back and curved top with the Spanish feet and ball turnings of stretcher that are definitively William and Mary. Scorned by the *nouveau*, such pieces are highly valued by the *cognoscente*.

Making up a subdivision of the William and Mary style are pieces dominated by spiral turnings, used in this case on a chair employed for watching cockfights. Users would straddle it and rest their arms on the top, which also opened to contain betting money. Walnut.

A lovely example of the use of trumpet legs on a ladies' writing desk. But the straight stretchers are wrong—either replacements or a variation in a Victorian reproduction.

A gem of William and Mary that features heavy spiral-turned legs, curved stretchers, tear-drop pulls, and richly inlaid veneer. Can be used as a dressing table or desk.

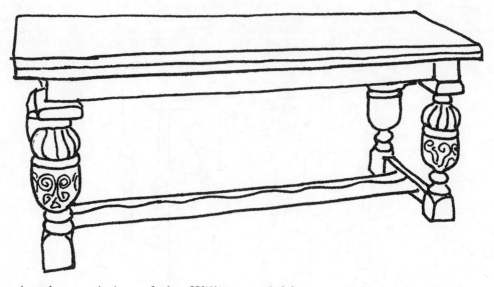

Another variation of the William and Mary period are the massive turned legs on this refectory table, as heavy, long dining tables of this kind are called.

When bun feet are elongated in the manner shown here, they are called turnip feet. The chest of drawers sits on a separate stand. Another transitional piece, as the drawers certainly have the simple serenity of the Queen Anne style.

In the early 1700s some William and Mary highboys were made in New England by emigrant English cabinetmakers, in either cherry or walnut wood. Once again the top of this one has the austerity of Queen Anne, the bottom the richness of William and Mary.

An early William and Mary piece consisting of a doored cabinet fitted with drawers and a center cupboard resting on a stand with spiral-turned legs and curved stretchers. As nice as ice.

An inferior Victorian reproduction of a library table for which the most that can be said is that it is *reminiscent* of William and Mary. There are a great many such pieces on the market.

This English Victorian reproduction of a William and Mary highboy, however, is a faithful one and can only be told from an original piece by minute examination of the interior workmanship.

WELSH "CUPBOARDS," 1650–1830

A popular English country piece

The term Welsh "cupboard" is a popular misnomer for a dresser which is, in fact, a sideboard with open shelves over it for the display of china, pewter, or other eating utensils. Undoubtedly the loose usage has come about from the fact that the sideboard usually has drawers in the center and cupboards on either side of them, or sometimes consists of three or four cupboards in a row.

It is also a mystery as to why these dressers are referred to as Welsh, since they were just as popular all over England, as well the rest of Europe. However, few were made in the American colonies, where narrower true cupboards with doors on both the top and bottom were preferred.

Invariably country-made by rural carpenters and furniture makers, they have been dated over a period of two hundred years, beginning in the late 1600s. They are probably still being made.

Early Welsh dresser made of oak, with Jacobean-style drawer fronts and shelf instead of stretchers. This was found in central England, where such pieces were just as popular as in Wales.

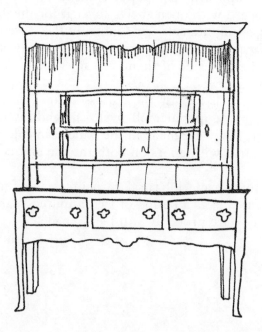

This walnut dresser from the Queen Anne era has the straight legs typical of the period, and worn-down pad feet, which indicate its age and therefore establish it as authentic. The doored compartments on either side are called jelly cupboards.

A high dresser with shelf instead of stretcher is typical of the kind of furniture for which the term "Georgian" was invented. It has an early-English look to it but is not definitely of any of the styles of the era.

The reason it is difficult to identify Welsh dressers as being of any particular style is that they weren't made in fashionable London cabinet shops, but by local craftsmen who just had a general idea of what one should look like.

This Welsh dresser was actually found in Llarghn, Wales, but even so there is no particular Welsh style. In this one the lower area is filled with cupboards and drawers.

Even this piece, built of golden oak, is called a Welsh dresser, though it was made in the early 1900s in Chicago.

QUEEN ANNE, 1700–50

Like swans on a lake

The Queen Anne style is always easily identified by the simple, graceful curves of its unadorned legs reminiscent of a swan's neck stretched high at attention. The effect this has when such legs are supporting a massive chest of drawers is to lift them off the floor to a stance that is eternally poised in space—once again, like swans gliding by on still water.

Historically Queen Anne was the first of English styles to differ from the heavy boxlike furniture that filled the castles of the Middle Ages. It was the first movable furniture of the Mercantile Era, a period that began around 1700 and lasted through the eighteenth century.

The wood used in England was walnut, often inlaid and veneered with fancy-grained walnut veneers cut from burls of the tree. In America, walnut was also used but not as often as cherry and maple.

Confident, dignified, well-bred, and quietly unassuming describe this flat-topped highboy in maple, with a chestnut back containing an inscription revealing that it was made in New England by a British-trained craftsman in the early 1700s. Unusually bold apron.

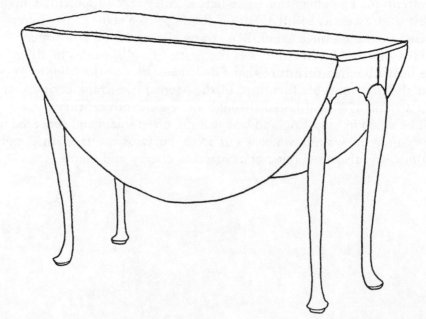

When the leaves of this table are put up and rest on its swing-out legs, the top is perfectly round. The legs are slightly heavy at the top but still have great style. Honduras mahogany. Made in England circa 1810.

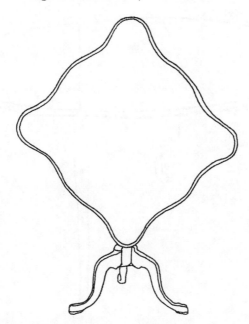

With an exciting flame-grain top of Honduras mahogany, this tilt-top
table has serpentine edges and classical snake-feet legs. Late eighteenth
century, English-made.

Usually called a sideboard in the United States, the English term for this
piece is a dressing table. Its classical lines and the fact that it is made of
oak show that it is a very early piece. But the same piece also is found in
Honduras mahogany.

Straightish legs and a gentle apron are characteristic of early Queen Anne tables like this one. The frames of these tables, which include unseen parts of the swing legs, are usually made of oak, and the mechanism is remarkably strong, even in the oldest ones.

This triple-backed settee in English walnut is a remarkable transitional piece. The tops of the back are in William and Mary style, and the slat backs are not fully developed, but the rest is all Queen Anne.

A classic lowboy design used as a sideboard in a dining room or library. These were commonly reproduced in England during the Victorian era, often in walnut due to a shortage of Honduras mahogany.

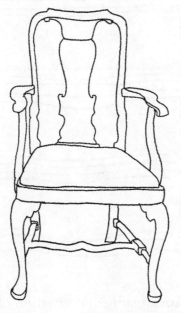

Late Queen Anne dining chair, the armchair of a set of six or eight. The beginnings of the style Chippendale made his own can be seen in the slight carving on the knee-tops.

A Victorian reproduction of a Queen Anne corner chair that lacks most of the style of the original design because of modifications of the back slats and the knees.

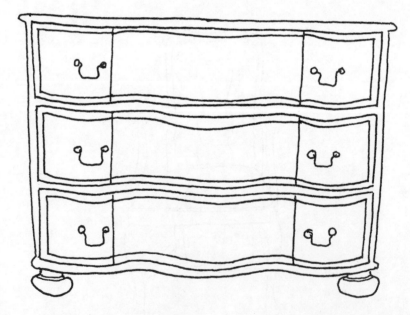

Nice, wide bun feet are an authentic variation of the Queen Anne style as shown in this softly curved block-front chest of drawers. The lacquered front with Chinese-motif decoration is also authentic if rare. Lacquered fronts became common in Chippendale furniture.

Tilt-top tea tables have always been an English favorite, as seen in this piece with a bird-cage–tilting mechanism for greater stability. Multicurved dish tops were also common, as were the snake feet.

Queen Anne legs without the knees are not considered defective but are deemed country-made, a very desirable variation that has much charm. A parallel to the great charm of the country-made Provençal variation of Louis XV in France.

The broken arch top of this bookcase is typical of Queen Anne pieces
made in the early 1700s in New England by young cabinet makers and
apprentices who moved here from England. The Spanish feet of the
William and Mary style are an interesting variation on the otherwise
classic lowboy beneath.

A low bookcase with good bracket feet, typical of the Queen Anne style,
and glass-window doors with separate panes. Also called a breakfront
because the center section stands out from the side sections.

The wings on the sides of this chair were supposed to protect your head from drafts while sitting around your castle or keep. This dates from the late 1700s, and the "Frenchification" of that time is apparent in the modeling of the legs. A piece that is still popular today.

The top of this highboy is called a split bonnet, as opposed to the plain or solid bonnets, or the split-arch bonnets also seen. A classic example of good proportions. As this was made in America, cherry was substituted for the mahogany used in England.

Fine "oyster" walnut sheets much thicker than veneer were used on the drawer fronts of this chest from the early 1700s. Split tear-drop pulls were a common variation. Originally had round bun feet, but these were weak and often had to be replaced with brackets like these.

Fine American broken-arch bonnet crowns this highboy with fan-carved central drawer at top. Classic Queen Anne in spite of the shield drawer pulls of the Chippendale period. A common overlap of the two styles that occurred before Chippendale's style book defined the difference.

An American-made tea table in perfect country Queen Anne style (no knees on the tops of legs). Made of solid tiger-figured maple, which indicates its New England origin. (Cherry ones are from Pennsylvania or western New York.) A gentle gem of a piece.

An especially graceful settee with three chair backs and "shepherd crook" arms at the sides. Made of Honduras mahogany in England circa 1780.

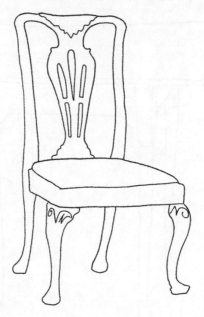

A good solid Queen Anne chair that shows the beginning of the "French-ification" (in the pierced back and slight carving on the knees) that leads toward the Chippendale style.

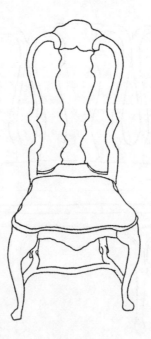

A "fancy" or bedroom chair covered with inlaid pieces of varicolored woods. An individual piece as opposed to the usual dining table sets of six or eight chairs that were often made of Honduras mahogany.

Exceptionally high and bold knees on these cabriol legs are early, fairly rare, and very desirable. A two-piece top and molded edges make this a simple, classic piece.

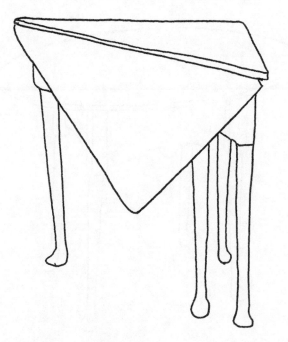

Sometimes called a handkerchief table, this one fits out of the way in a corner of a room, ready to be pulled out for tea or card playing. Fine, thin straight legs make it a shining example of country Queen Anne.

Corner table opened with a leaf that rests on a swing leg in the rear. Honduras mahogany, made in England. Rare in America.

A rare and precious American-made tea table with splayed country-style straight legs. Made in maple or cherry and often covered with dark red paint, if found in original condition. Paint usually worn off the top.

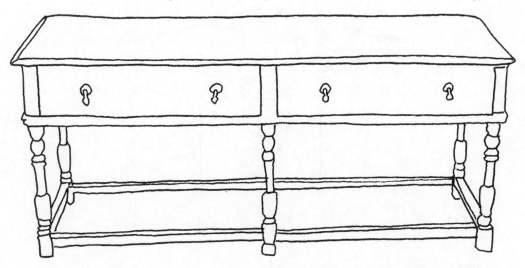

Some very early pieces like this are classified as Queen Anne, even though they retain the turned legs and stretcher base from the William and Mary period. But tear-drop pulls and diamond escutcheon are very typical of Queen Anne. The feet were rotted by a dirt floor and have been evened off. Probably pre-1700.

The high knees and straight legs identify this gaming table as coming from Connecticut, Rhode Island, or southeastern Massachusetts, where walnut and cherry were the usual woods. Tables made of Honduras mahogany can be assumed to be English.

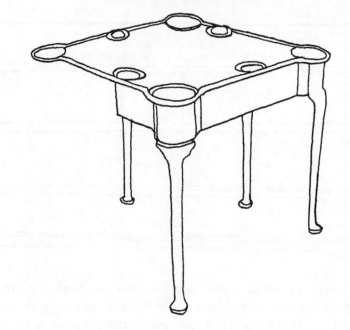

When not in use, these tables were kept against a wall with the top folded down. Here, seen opened, one swing leg supports half of the top, revealing corner pockets used to hold money or chips.

Flat-topped highboys—that is, those without a bonnet sitting on top— were popular in southern Vermont, New Hampshire, and Maine, where bonnets were considered frivolous by rock-farm Yankees. An almost Shaker simplicity. Wide map drawer at top for a surveyor.

Conventional New England Queen Anne highboy—very high—from a governor's mansion. Unusual features include two fan carvings on the base. Tiger maple was used for special pieces such as this.

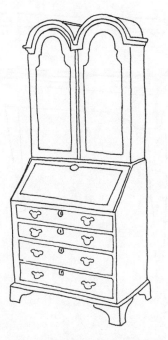

"Double-dome" is the term used for this style of secretary, the American name for a slant-front desk surmounted by a bookcase. The English term for these pieces is "bureau-bookcase."

Made in England in the mid-1700s, this double-dome bureau-bookcase has rare glass doors, which were probably added in the early 1800s.

An American-made tray-top tea table that demonstrates how closely the cabinetmakers who emigrated from England in the mid-1700s stuck to the designs they learned back home. Found all over the Northeast.

A standard-design Queen Anne settee that could have been made either in England or America from 1700 to 1765. All such pieces have to be completely reupholstered, usually with a faithful copy of the original brocade fabric.

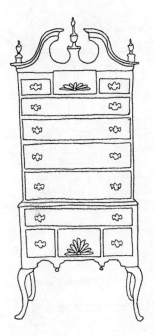

This broken-arch highboy with two carved fans is such a classic design that it has been duplicated every year since the first one was made. This one, in the Massachusetts manner (two fans), was handmade in Boston circa 1850.

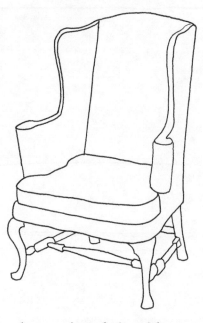

This classic Queen Anne wing chair with a strong stretcher base has become a classic style that is still being widely produced by cabinet shops all along the East Coast.

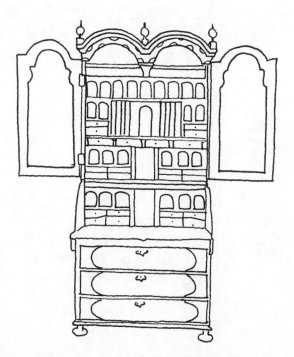

A wonderfully ornate but perfectly styled double-dome bureau bookcase ("secretary" in U.S. usage), this was made in England circa 1730. All exterior surfaces are lacquered and decorated in the Chinese manner copied from Chinese screens brought back by trading ships.

A made-in-England breakfront for china and linens that is veneered with fancy burl walnut. A magnificent piece, but not for the average home.

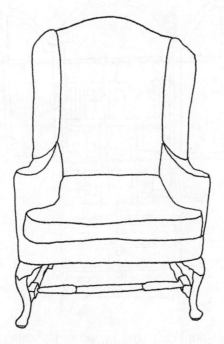

Block and turned stretchers are the Massachusetts hallmark of this classic example of a Queen Anne wing chair.

Classic double-dome English-made Queen Anne bureau-bookcase. For such large pieces, native walnut was used as often as Honduras mahogany. Circa 1710.

A single-dome bureau-bookcase that is one of the most popular pieces of furniture ever made because of the way it combines grace of line with superb usefulness.

CHIPPENDALE, 1740–70

*The perfect combination of English and French designs
—with a dash of Chinese*

The key to understanding the style we call Chippendale is that it is basically Queen Anne furniture with applied decoration "in the French manner." At least, that is how Thomas Chippendale himself described it in his book of designs that he published for sale to other cabinetmakers who wanted to know what was popular at the time in London.

In other words the style of Chippendale did not spring full blown from Chippendale's head, but grew out of the taste of the bustling middle class of the time in the city that was at the heart of the emerging British Empire. And what these Englishmen were impressed with was the decorativeness of the "artistic French" in Paris across the Channel. And Chippendale's *Gentleman's and Cabinet-Makers Directory* codified this taste for all time, allowing it to be reproduced in British outposts of empire all around the world and especially in their American colonies.

However, the enduring popularity of this style cannot only be credited to good information distribution; it also surely rests on the fact that it combines the artistic thrust of two cultures—French and English—the two most powerful and expansive ones of the eighteenth century.

In addition Chippendale is certainly the most eclectic of the popular styles of the eighteenth century—the golden century of furniture design. To be sure, its main delights are the addition of acanthus leaves to the knee of the Queen Anne leg and a ball-and-claw to its foot. But we also have ribbon carving on the backs of chairs, some square fluted legs, some round reeded legs reminiscent of Louis XVI, and much latticework in the Chinese manner—as a result of Britain's China Trade. (In fact, many pieces in the Chippendale style were made in China for export to London.)

Almost all Chippendale is made of Honduras mahogany, the ideal wood for making furniture because it combines strength with colorful grain and is easy to carve. It had just become available from British Honduras.

By far the most Chippendale furniture sold today was made in the Victorian era in England and is called "Centennial". But since it was also made of Honduras mahogany and was so carefully crafted, it is difficult to tell from the original "of the period" pieces. And, of course, it has been continuously made for the last two hundred years by cabinet shops in every civilized country in the world.

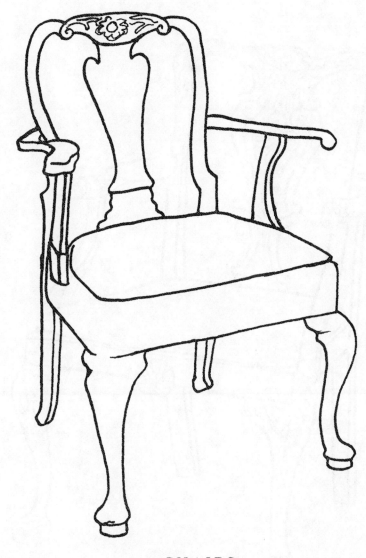

CHAIRS

This basically Queen Anne chair is placed at the opening of this Chippendale section because by comparing it with the next chair it illustrates how the transition from Queen Anne to Chippendale occurred. The legs have become bolder than is usual in Queen Anne. Ornamental carving has been introduced on the rail. The splat back is a little more ornate and has higher wings. But the whole chair is still relatively austere in comparison to . . .

. . . this chair in the full-blown Chippendale style. The only structural change is the higher corners of the back. But observe the decorative carving across the rail, an ornately carved splat, carving on the arms and knees of the legs, and ball-and-claw feet. In all a decorative "Frenchification" of the basic Queen Anne design.

Of all furniture styles, the one we call Chippendale is certainly the most
eclectic and already included many variations by the time Chippendale
published his book of designs. These chairs have even more pointed corners, thin carved splats inspired by Roman designs, and square fluted
legs which had replaced the Queen Anne cabriol legs by the time Chippendale's design book came out.

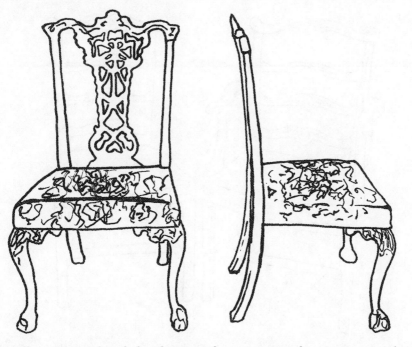

An excellent example of the degree of ornateness that we expect in the
Chippendale style, a worldly richness.

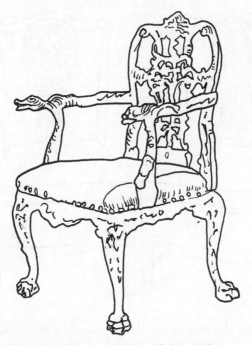

But this chair is a gross exaggeration of the richness of French decoration
—including ball-and-paw feet on all four legs and bird-head handles on
the arms. It is, of course, not a real Chippendale piece, but a Victorian
fantasy made for some American robber baron to scare his children with.
Ah, folly, thy name is excess.

In contrast Chippendale also includes the quiet gracefullness of these
ribbon-back chairs with their thin fluted square legs.

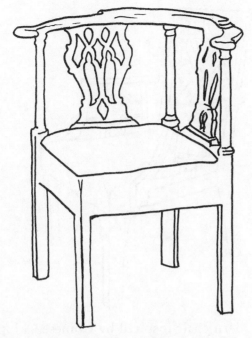

The Chippendale square leg was not always fluted as it is in this typical Chippendale corner chair. And except for the carved splat, this one is remakable, simple, and clean in its design, which only demonstrates the range we find in this style.

Another important part of the Chippendale style is the chairs with backs reminiscent of Chinese latticework, inspired by objects brought home from China by Britain's great trading fleet of the middle 1700s.

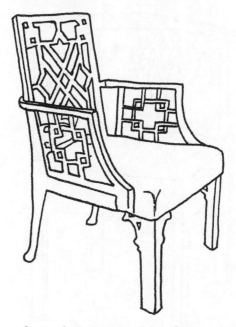

This is actually a modern chair inspired by Chinese Chippendale.

And these are Victorian reproductions faithfully copied from Chippendale's book of designs.

A good example of ribbon-back carving, this chair is not in Chippendale's design book. It was made in Pennsylvania by a good country cabinetmaker who was inspired by examples he saw in the big city of Philadelphia.

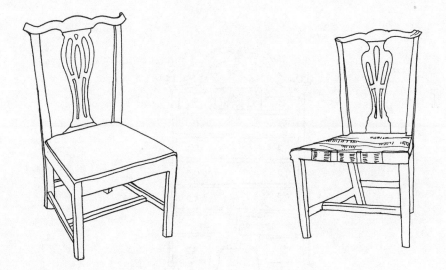

These chairs are country Chippendale, a simplified version of the style. Country Chippendale chairs were widely made in America from 1750 through the 1800s by country cabinetmakers—actually carpenters who made furniture in the winter months when it was too cold to work outside.

CHESTS

A classic four-drawer Chippendale chest of drawers for a gentleman's bedroom. The identifying feature is the shape of the leg, which is based on a double or O.G. curve—i.e., concave above and convex below. Although the escutcheons are similar to those used in Hepplewhite, they first came into use in the Chippendale style.

The range of what is possible in Chippendale is well illustrated in this highboy and the following one. This English piece has everything: the bonnet top, high finials, the shield escutcheons, a fan, apron finials, and ball-and-claw feet.

An austere Early American version, made in New Hampshire around 1750, has the two fans, the ball-and-claw feet, but simple aprons, no finials, and a flat top. As cabinetmakers considered highboys their masterpieces, no two are exactly alike, although they are in the Chippendale manner.

Fine flame-grain Honduras mahogany was often used in Chippendale, as in this desk with nice O.G.-curve legs. In this piece, the elements on the desktop are upside down. Small drawers were usually on the bottom with cubbyholes on top of them. Not a fault—in fact, an interesting feature.

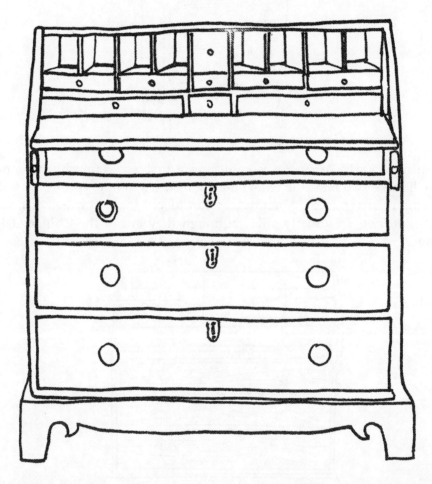

As with highboys, no two slant-front Chippendale desks are exactly alike. Chippendale's design book may have set certain standards, but good cabinetmakers are an independent breed. However, the lines of this desk are close to the standard product with graduated drawers and cubbyholes and small drawers inside. The wooden knobs on this piece are replacements put on in the middle 1800s, the Empire period in the United States, to modernize the piece. However, they can easily be replaced by reproduction brasses.

Narrower Chippendale desks like this one are very desirable as ladies' desks because they take up less space in rooms that can't take the bulk of a full-sized desk. These narrow desks are an American variation and were mostly made in New England of maple with an interesting grain, such as curly or tiger maple.

A standard ball-and-claw foot slant-front Chippendale desk with a gentle oxbow front. American made, circa 1790.

The most popular of all Chippendale desks are the ones with block-front drawers, most often made in Rhode Island. Original pieces are worth as much as a Rolls-Royce. But naturally the style has been widely copied and is still being carefully made by fine cabinetmakers in New England.

This fine Chippendale partners' desk is so called because it has the same drawer on the other side. The charming idea was, of course, that partners in a business should have no secrets from each other.

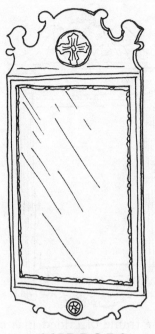

MIRRORS

Early Chippendale fretwork mirror still displaying much of the gentle curvaceousness of the preceding Queen Anne period.

A later and more typical pierced-scroll fretwork mirror in the usual thinly cut Honduras mahogany. It just looks more French—which was the whole idea of Chippendale.

Greek-temple-style mirror frame of gilded plaster-of-Paris on a wooden understructure. The same broken pediment scroll top, or bonnet, as used on highboys. More testimony that the term Chippendale means more an era than a style, and a good reason for referring to the mirror with the ambiguous term "George I."

SECRETARIES & VARIATIONS

Although the term "secretary" is now understood by all, Chippendale originally used the term "bureau-bookcase" for such pieces, and the English still do. So do some interior decorators who are trying to impress you. Here a standard design with lattice over glass in the bookcase doors, unusual square feet.

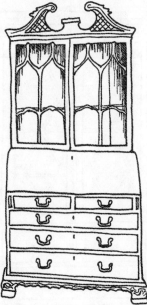

Scroll-top pediments are most usual on Chippendale secretaries, but the lattice shown here is unusual. The carving on an O.G.-footed base has an Irish look but is not definitive.

A fine example of an American-made Chippendale secretary with the brass finials found in pieces made around Boston. Oxbow front and O.G. feet make this a highly desirable piece. The oval drawer pulls were frequently used on such American pieces.

A Chippendale bookcase with drawers under it is authentic enough in style and proportions, but rare.

Ah, eclecticism, thy name is Chippendale! Fine legs with ball-and-claw feet. But, then, Irish-style carving on the apron, Queen Anne teardrop drawer pulls, Gothic arches in the latticework, and a French fence on top. Is this interesting, or not pure enough? *Chacun à son goût!*

A close cousin of the secretary is this beautifully proportioned break-front combining drawers, cupboards, and bookshelves behind latticed glass doors. The term "breakfront" comes from the fact that the center section comes out six or seven inches from the side sections. Flame-grain Honduras mahogany, of course.

A black-lacquered Chippendale secretary with chinoiserie decoration. The desk and O.G. legs are pure Chippendale, but the double bonnet has a look left over from Queen Anne, and the lacquer finish is also borrowed from that style. Definitely made in England, since lacquer was never used in the American colonies.

Lacquered with a dark red finish and decorated in the Chinese style, this Chippendale bookcase is a very successful design and is highly sought-after.

This Chippendale display cabinet is an unusual piece with fine spade-footed Marlborough legs, but the decoration on the top is fussy and the apron is out of touch with the fine proportions of the rest of the piece.

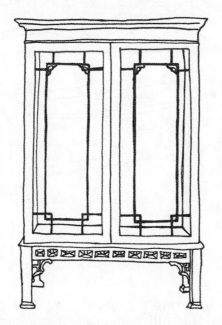

A Chippendale china cabinet that goes as far into the Chinese style as you can go.

TABLES

A high-kneed Chippendale gaming table with pockets for chips or cash. In a piece like this, the smaller paw feet seen here are preferable to the usual ball and claw. Many reproductions of this piece were made in England during the Victorian era.

The ubiquitous butler's tray is probably the most reproduced piece of furniture of all time. It is still being made by cabinetmakers all over the world. The best, of Honduras mahogany, can only be told from the originals by signs of wear—and that can be faked too.

A classic Chippendale serving table with the square Marlborough legs and typical escutcheons. How clean and simple compared to other highly decorated Chippendale pieces. The drawer fronts look like Sheraton, but Chippendale this piece surely is.

The square feet on the square legs of this card table are the beginning of the Chinese influence, as are the leg brackets. The three-piece top of this table unfolds and swings around to make a dining-sized table. With struck brass escutcheons and of Honduras mahogany.

Rather bolder and more intricate carving characterize the Irish variation of the Chippendale style as seen in this center table for a library or drawing room. The Irish version of the paw foot is called knucklebone.

The shaped apron of this tea table is also typical of Irish Chippendale. The concave "dish" top is carved out of a solid piece of Honduras mahogany. Elongated knee and knucklefoot.

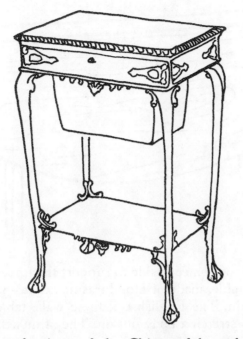

Most Victorian reproductions of the Chippendale style were faithful copies based on Chippendale's book of designs. So this sewing table is unusual in that it is an interpretation of the style that adds some extra flourishes—such as the curly leg braces and the teardrops on the apron and shelf—which are not really successful.

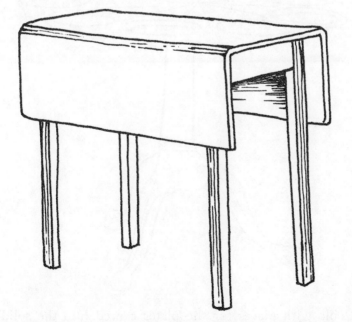

The fluted Marlborough legs may define this drop-leaf table as Chippendale, but it is a stark, cold piece indeed. It is a country cabinetmaker's piece made in New England around 1780.

Two legs swing out on each side to support the leaves of this grand oval-topped dining table, made of Honduras mahogany with flamboyant figures in the grain. The English call these wake tables because they are long enough to stretch a body out on. They think that's funny!

A supper table with places for the plates carved into the solid top of Honduras mahogany. Ball-and-claw feet, but the heavy pedestal is a complete failure. Another bad Victorian reproduction—but not out of Chippendale's design book.

Made in America, circa 1750, this walnut tilt-top table has a clumsy base and legs far heavier than needed. But American examples of Chippendale that can be authenticated are highly valued, no matter what.

This is a tea table with Marlborough legs and porringer-shaped corners. Another stark Chippendale design, but one that comes off well.

Just for comparison to pieces with an integrated design, this tilt-top tea table has a piecrust top, Queen Anne snake feet, and a heavy, ugly center post. The best that can be said of it is that it is made of Honduras mahogany.

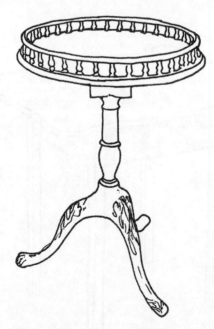

Because of the fence-edged top and carving on the knees of the legs, some people have the nerve to offer a design mess like this table as Chippendale. It is, of course, a Victorian misadventure to be scorned by the *cognoscente*.

Right out of Chippendale's design book, this is a side table that turns into a flight of stairs for getting books from high library shelves. A wonderful piece of furniture that is still being accurately reproduced.

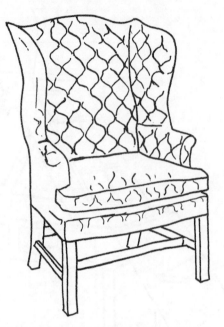

UPHOLSTERED PIECES

The most popular and comfortable chair of all time is certainly an upholstered Chippendale wing chair such as this one with fluted square legs in the Marlborough manner.

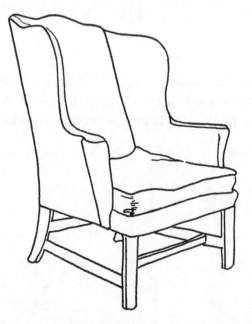

The wings were invented to prevent drafts from giving you a cold while sitting around in a drafty old English manor house. Down filling was used for extra coziness. All original examples would have to be completely reglued and reupholstered.

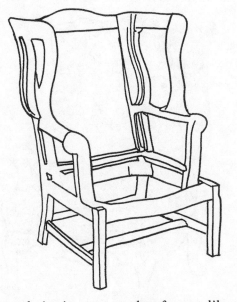

The demand for these chairs is so great that frames like this one are still being made by many cabinetmakers around the world. The fluted legs and stretchers are mahogany; the rest are usually maple and oak. The frame is sent to an upholsterer, where buyers choose the fabric they want.

Upholstered chairs in the ornate version of Chippendale often come with all four legs carved. This one of walnut has paw feet.

Ball-and-claw feet in the front and Queen Anne pad feet in the back of this Irish Chippendale wing chair are not an unusual combination. The carving on the apron indicates the Irish origin of this chair.

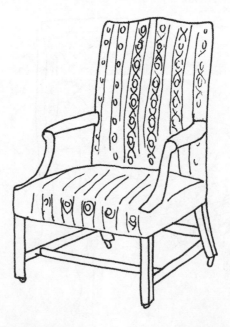

Roomy Chippendale chairs like this were called lolling chairs—popular in private libraries and public hotel lobbies. They were often mounted on coasters for easy moving.

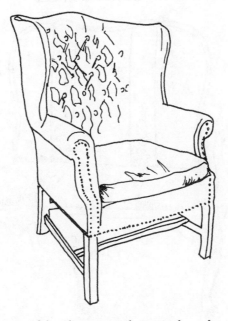

Black- or burgundy-stained leather was also employed to cover Chippendale wing chairs for use in libraries and men's clubs. Lots of brass-headed
nails were used for decoration.

In the Chippendale era, it seemed obvious that two chair frames could be
put together to make a wider seat that they called a settee. The heaviness
of the legs and large ball-and-claw feet are an exaggeration revealing that
this is a Victorian reproduction.

Carved eagle heads grace the arms of this well-proportioned settee that overcomes the "two chairs glued together" look of most Chippendale settees. Good fans on the apron and acanthus leaves on the knees give a fine heavy Chippendale look.

The fully upholstered camel back on this settee make it look almost like a couch, which it would be without the two middle legs. This became a reality in . . .

This classic camel-back sofa is a famous and still popular Chippendale design with square, fluted Marlborough legs.

Chippendale camel-back sofas are also found with the ornate carved knee and ball-and-claw foot.

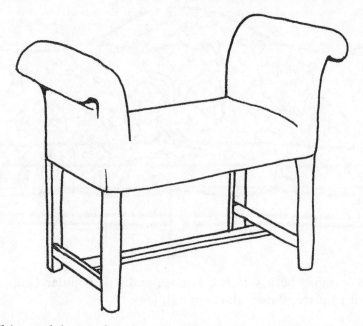

This Chippendale window bench with Marlborough legs is an interesting piece but one that has only rarely been reproduced.

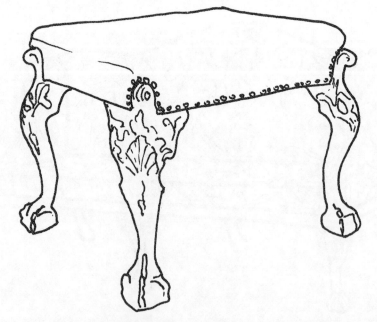

The essence of Chippendale's concept of furniture "in the French manner" is displayed in this footstool used as a small sitting stool as well. Fan carving on knee and Chinese-inspired claw-on-ball foot.

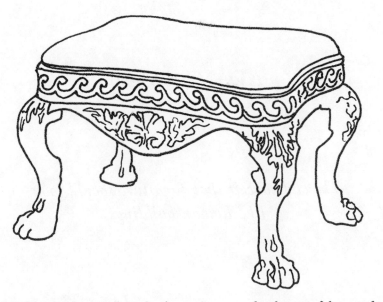

The paw feet and acanthus leaf carving on the knee of leg and apron, gilded Greek frieze on serpentine top give a French Baroque richness to this Chippendale foot or sitting stool.

This Victorian reproduction of a Chippendale sitting stool was made from Chippendale's design book with the result that it is the most authentic of the three stools shown here.

ADAM, 1765–90

*The odd conceit that furniture should look
like Roman buildings*

In 1719 English archaeologists discovered and began to excavate the ruins of the ancient Roman city of Herculaneum—and later Pompeii in 1756.

Well, true to their xenophilic nature, this delighted everybody in England. Each new discovery was reported in the newspapers, and lecturers came back from Italy to draw crowds that filled the halls of academe.

And as architects and interior designers are always looking for something new to please their newly wealthy customers—and England was full of such wealth at that time of mercantile expansion—two brothers named Adam pounced upon the idea that truly tasteful and classy furniture should look like Roman temples—or at least bathing houses.

So, using a lot of expensive satinwood and olive green inlays, they proceeded with their idea and got away with it. They not only designed houses for their clients, but everything that went inside of them. And they were a big success—with half the craftsmen in England working for them on lighting, table service, carpets, drapes, and, of course, furniture. In fact, even Mr. Hepplewhite worked for them before he struck out on his own with his far more reasonable style based on the same Roman lines and proportions.

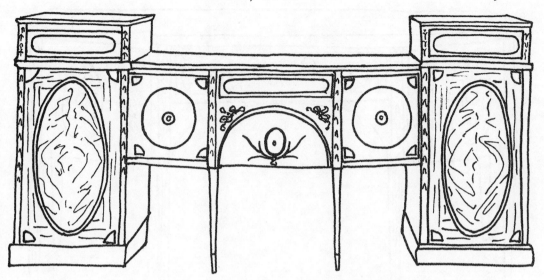

Looking somewhat like a row of buildings—in ancient Rome, of course—
this sideboard epitomizes the Adam style. The basic wood is lightly
stained mahogany inlaid with pale satinwood.

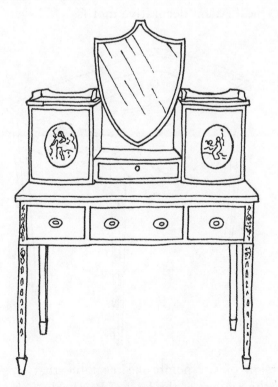

As noted the architectural look of the Adam style was inspired by the
discovery of the ruins of Pompeii and Herculaneum in the early 1700s.
Characteristic of the style are the thin, square-tapered legs supporting
this no-frills lady's dressing table.

Most successful of the Adam designs were the sideboards that Hepplewhite would take with him for the work that bears his name. Garlands and ovals are typical Adam decorative motifs.

The Adam version of the pembroke tea table that was originated by Chippendale at the request of the Earl of Pembroke, who liked his tables to have their tops wider than their leaves. The result was that the legs were farther apart to give the table more stability on uneven floors—thereby spilling less tea.

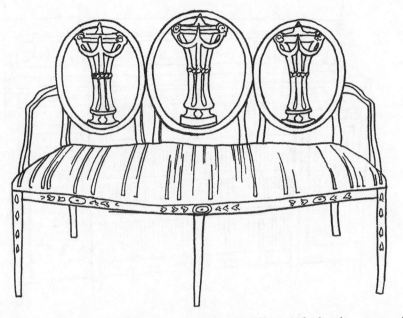

Ah, fragility, thy name is Adam, as in this spindly triple-back settee with ribbon-carved splats. The only unbroken pieces of the period are in museums, and hardly any reproductions were made in Victorian England, while Queen Anne and Chippendale were so vigorously being reproduced.

Another incredible delicate Adam settee that features hand-painted portraits in the centers of the backs. These were common. Some were made by a Swiss painter named Angelica Kauffmann. Those that were made by one of her imitators are said to be "in the manner of Angelica Kauffmann."

A satinwood bookcase in the manner of the Adam brothers with consid-
erable hand-painted decoration in the manner of Angelica Kauffmann.

A demilune commode in the Adam style is profusely decorated with
garlands in the Roman manner and two fine paintings in the Angelica
Kauffmann manner, featuring romantic figures in sylvan backgrounds—
usually drawn from tales in Greek mythology.

The fine inlay work on these Adam side cabinets can't make up for the basic dumbness of the idea that furniture should imitate Roman buildings—and rest on square, clumsy legs.

Another less-than-brilliant Adam idea was to make a knife box out of a Greek urn of turned mahogany inlaid with satinwood. These were intended to stand on each end of a sideboard.

Marble tops were often put on small corner cabinets heavily decorated with inlaid garlands and oval paintings in the manner of Angelica Kauffmann. The surfaces of Adam furniture are always vastly superior to their lines. Note the clumsy legs on this piece.

A mirror from the Adam period is naturally decorated with garlands and urns but still manages to look like a building sitting firmly on the ground.

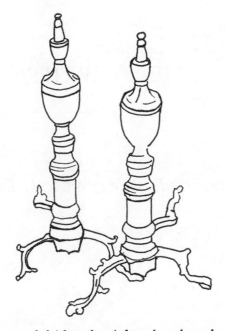

Probably the most successful idea the Adam brothers had was to use the Greek urn motif for andirons—an idea which has lasted into the present.

Looking like an American dry sink, this unusual Adam piece is called a credence, a transitional design on its way to becoming a sideboard.

HEPPLEWHITE

The most "successful" style of all truly English furniture

Thin tapered legs are the hallmark of the style that George Hepplewhite developed from the flat-headed designs of the Adam brothers, who had drawn their inspiration from the Roman ruins excavated in Italy during the first half of the eighteenth century.

Best known of the Hepplewhite designs are the chairs which have delicate backs in the shapes of shields, ovals, hearts, wheels, and one with a camel-hump back. But just as popular are the sideboards that have a very light and airy look, almost as if they were floating.

So where the Adam brothers failed, Hepplewhite succeeded in turning the proportions of ancient Rome into a valid and important style of furniture that is at the same time delicate and dignified, almost official-looking.

Like Chippendale, Hepplewhite also published the designs of the furniture he and his fellow cabinetmakers were selling at the time. And since this was a great success, the Hepplewhite style was also "finalized" by it. This means that since 1788, when the catalogue was published, until today, cabinetmakers have been faithfully reproducing it without experimentation or variation.

As a result, Hepplewhite is the purest style of furniture that we have. It is even purer than Chippendale since Chippendale was transitional pieces from Queen Anne and there are also Irish and Philadelphia variations of it.

Thus many designers consider Hepplewhite the most *successful* of all furniture styles. Because it didn't lend itself to the variations that would have created transitional pieces to either the Adam style that came before it or the Sheraton style that followed.

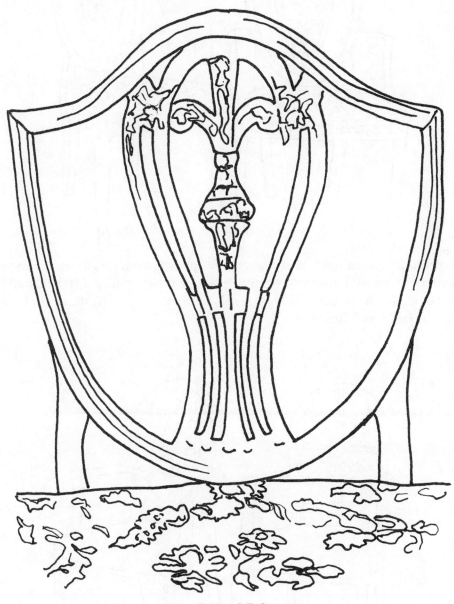

CHAIRS

Hepplewhite chairs are easily recognized by their delicate shield backs— marvelous feats of engineering in wood that make them far stronger than they look. The wood that makes them possible, of course, is Honduras mahogany, which has an amorphous grain that is strong in all directions, preventing it from very easily splitting under pressure.

Tapered legs with spade feet are most frequently seen on chairs, whereas the foot is usually absent on table legs and other pieces. Garlands and arches derive from the mid-eighteenth-century interest in the arts of ancient Greece and Rome.

Wheel-back Hepplewhite chairs were not as common as the ones with shields, but come right out of Hepplewhite's book of designs.

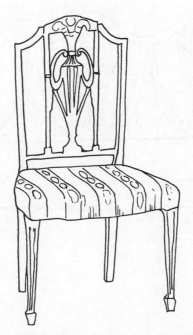

A rare Hepplewhite chair, because it has begun a transition to the Sheraton and Regency styles brought about by French influence. Transitional
elements are the straight verticals in the back and the fluted legs which
will soon become round.

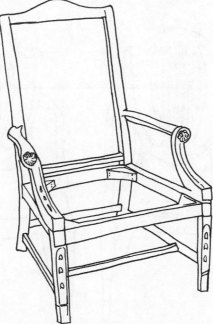

Frame for a Hepplewhite armchair of great simplicity. Compare to the
preceding Chippendale chairs with top wings and "overdecorated" cabriole legs. Note the absence of spade feet on the legs of almost all pieces
heavier than chairs.

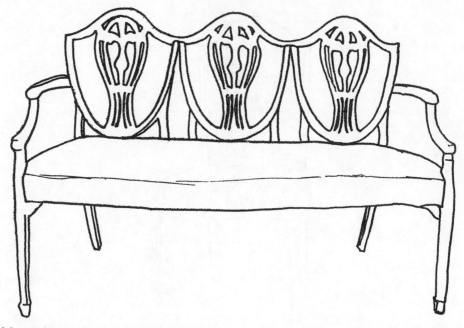

No eighteenth-century cabinetmaker could resist the wild surmise that if he put three chairs together he'd have a couch. Of course, what he actually got is called a settee, and without a center leg this one is sure to collapse the first time a grown man sits on it.

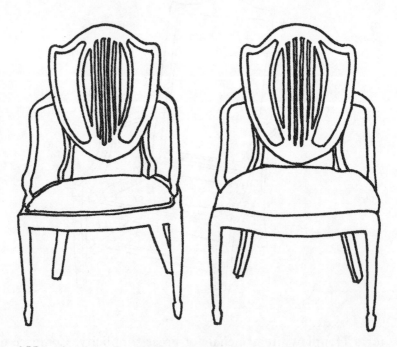

A pair of Hepplewhite fauteuil (open arms) side chairs made during the Victorian era in England with slip-in seats and uninteresting backs. The over-all heaviness misses the point of being Hepplewhite.

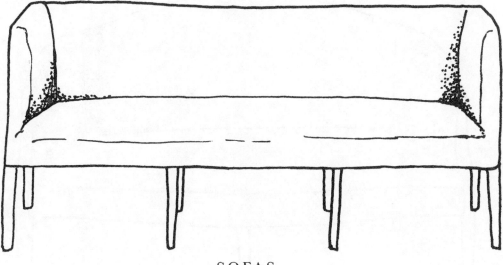

SOFAS

A straight-back Hepplewhite sofa. The severe rectangular lines are faithful to the designer's ideal of simplicity, but unfortunately the piece ends up looking like a long box—or floating coffin.

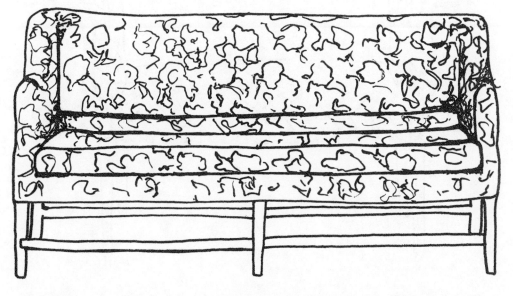

Stretchers running between the legs of this country-made version of a straight-back Hepplewhite sofa warm the design up considerably, and the floral design of the fabric helps, too.

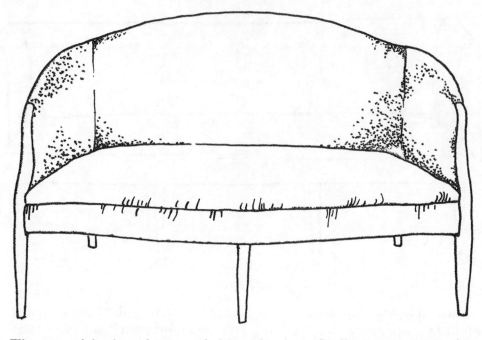

The curved back and arms of this sofa-settee finally return us to the gracefulness of the Hepplewhite idea while still retaining its simplicity.

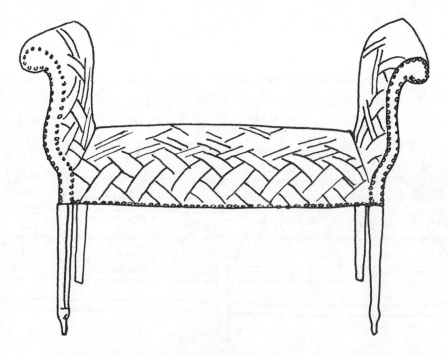

An unusual Hepplewhite window bench of the late 1700s that is transitional into the Sheraton style in the rounding of the thin tapered legs. Here again, we see the recurring French influence on English furniture.

CHESTS

Standard stock at any antiques import house are Hepplewhite chests of
drawers. Honduras mahogany veneers in flame grain, fine-line satinwood
inlays, struck brass oval drawer pulls, and the very special Hepplewhite
"French foot" that curves gently outward.

Most Hepplewhite chests are swell-front, but this one is gently serpentine. Wide bail pulls are an acceptable variation from the oval ones.

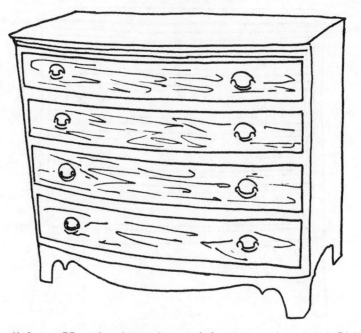

This swell-front Hepplewhite chest of drawers takes on a Chippendale look only because the curved French feet have been shortened four or five inches in a leveling-off procedure.

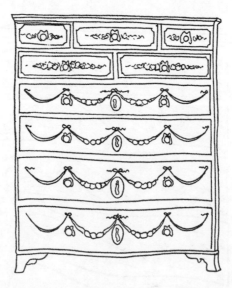

When the Hepplewhite style caught on in the United States during the 1920s and '30s, many very well-made reproductions came out of Grand Rapids. Most of the American pieces were painted a pale green and enthusiastically decorated with garlands and small scenes in the manner of Angelica Kauffmann. The short French foot is correct and works perfectly.

A taller than usual Hepplewhite chest made in New England in the middle 1800s. The wood was cherry, usually stained to look like mahogany in imitation of the English product.

An unusual twelve-drawer Hepplewhite chest of drawers with the look of a campaign chest, but without handles on the sides. The chest sits on separate frames and is made of beautifully grained Honduras mahogany.

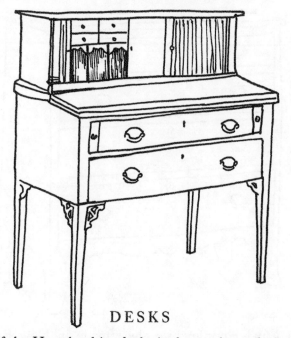

DESKS

Most typical of the Hepplewhite desks is the tambour desk—named after the sliding reed panels that cover the drawers. The top of this one folds out to rest on slide-out supports next to the drawer ends.

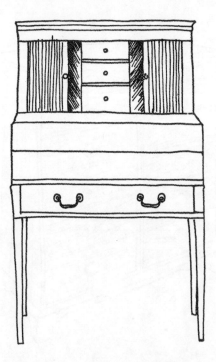

Fall-front tambour desk of flame-grain Honduras mahogany with alternate baille drawer pulls. Note that spade feet do not occur on these delicate pieces.

Forerunner of the golden-oak roll-top office desks of the early 1900s is this barrel-top tambour desk. Dark, figured mahogany and most typical oval drawer pulls.

No, this is not a sideboard shown here among desks by mistake. It just looks like a sideboard. The false drawer front falls forward to reveal a butler's desk full of small drawers and cubbyholes. Fine inlays and richly figured mahogany.

A more traditional butler's desk is here shown opened. When closed, it looks like a chest of drawers. The turned legs are definitely not Hepplewhite, but an encroachment of the coming Sheraton style in response to French influence.

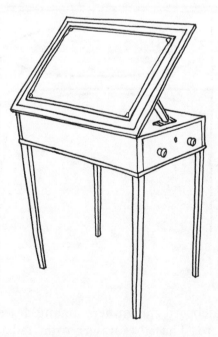

Architects desk with top that lowers to provide a table top. Single long, wide, deep drawer for holding plans.

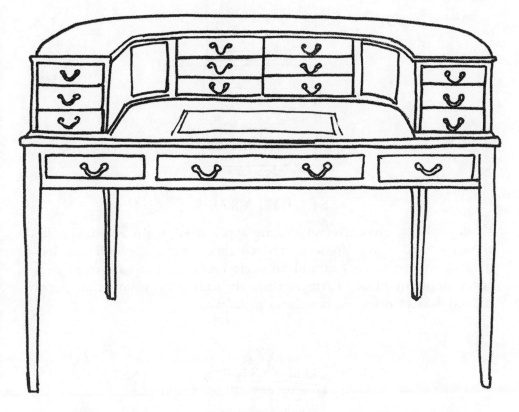

A magnificent Carlton House desk and drawing table. The center tilts up for use as a drawing board; a wide drawer holds large pieces of paper. Circa 1780. The same desk appears in the Sheraton style that follows Hepplewhite.

SECRETARIES

While all Hepplewhite secretaries are appreciated, the most popular are those crowned with swan-neck pediments such as this one with fine Hepplewhite-style French feet and an eagle inlaid on the slant-front desk cover. Superbly made in America shortly after the revolution of cherry stained dark to resemble Honduras mahogany.

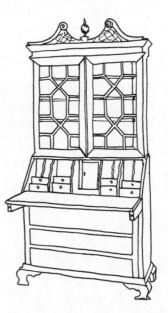

An example of the popular lattice pediment, though it is also, of course, a swan-neck. Feet of the desk are O.G. in the Chippendale style, but such transitional blends are quite common.

You can almost see the Greek or Roman temple behind this straight-edge broken-arch pediment. Decorated with blind fretwork and thin inlaid lines of satinwood. The O.G. feet that many of these pieces have is not as desirable as the Hepplewhite French foot.

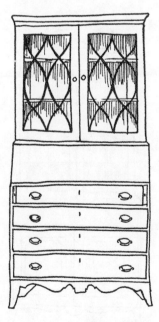

Simplified American versions of the Hepplewhite secretary were flat-topped in New England, made of cherry wood and without satinwood inlay striping. In the South—from Philadelphia down—they had the usual pediments. These are popular with Americana collectors.

This bow-arch Hepplewhite secretary was made in England and is considered to be under the Adam influence—for both the bow and brass
finials. But the base is definitely Hepplewhite.

Although it has a fine-bold broken-arch pediment, this piece is actually a
pretty fancy commode with a single drawer over a cabinet with two
drawers, though it could also be considered a library piece.

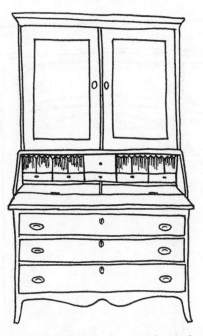

An early American Hepplewhite desk to which has been added a two-door bookcase in the much later simple American Empire style. The proportions work, but the difference between the top and bottom is so obvious that pieces like this are not highly valued. But with the top removed, you would have a fine cherry desk.

A fine example of early American Hepplewhite in cherry, this piece has fine inlays of satinwood, but it is not a secretary. It is called a linen press. It has fine French feet and brass finials.

SIDEBOARDS

Because the size of dining rooms has decreased since the early 1800s, small Hepplewhite sideboards are the most popular today. But even with a concave front, the proportions of this typical small one miss the grace of a "real" Hepplewhite sideboard.

However, this bow-front Hepplewhite sideboard has the width to make its proportions succeed—and also to make it one of the most popular pieces of furniture ever designed, especially in the United States, where it was widely reproduced in the 1920s and 1930s.

Another classic Hepplewhite sideboard, this one without the back apron of the previous one, has a decidedly classical look that is emphasized by the Adam proportions of the side cabinets . . . all pulled together by the camelback brass rail on the top.

An American-made Hepplewhite sideboard from the 1820s when the style was most popular with fine cabinetmakers around New York City and Philadelphia. Perfect proportions and flamboyant flame-grain Honduras mahogany.

Fanned arches under the center drawer of this Hepplewhite sideboard are once again a foretaste of the change over to the Sheraton style that followed Hepplewhite.

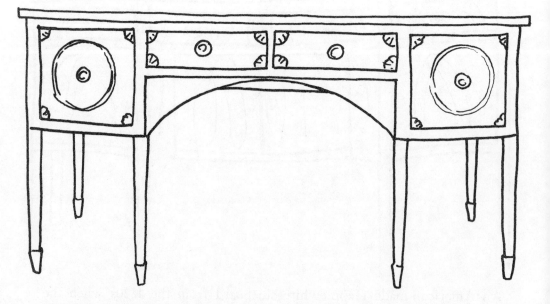

A dark and heavy Hepplewhite that begins to show the resurgence of the French influence that would lead to the Sheraton style replacing Hepplewhite.

A minisideboard called a server is perhaps the most successful piece of all Hepplewhite designs. This one is of satinwood with hand-painted Greek garlands and sylvan scene in the manner of Angelica Kauffmann on the top.

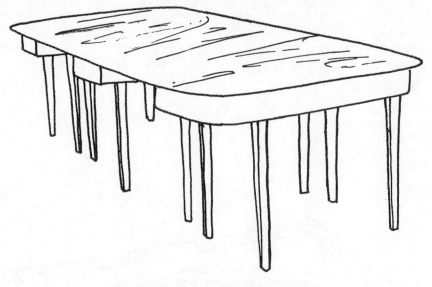

TABLES AND STANDS

This classic grand dining table in the Hepplewhite style is made up of three separate tables, the middle one having two drop leaves. The two end tables can also be joined for a smaller dining table. It is often called a banquet table and is made of wonderfully wide pieces of Honduras mahogany. Richly figured, fit for a duke.

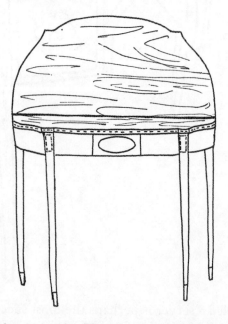

An ever popular classic in the Hepplewhite style is this collapsible card table. The back leaf either folds down frontward or is supported by the outside swing legs for the game of choice—preferably whist.

A rosewood gem of richly inlaid rosewood is this envelope or handkerchief table. The four triangles on the top flip out to rest on slip supports
and provide a larger card table.

Hepplewhite loved small tables with their tops wider than their leaves,
an idea suggested to him by one Lord Pembroke, for whom these tables
are naturally named. The legs and thin cross-stretchers are pure Hepplewhite. An eminently successful design that almost floats in the air.

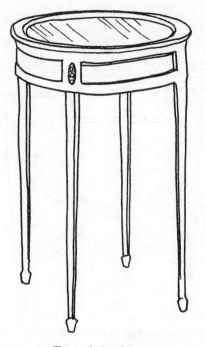

Pure Hepplewhite but very French-looking, this small, round table has a glass top and sides for displaying collections or curios. The name for it is a vitrine, from the Latin word for glass. Unusual tiny spade feet and satin strip inlay.

A two-tier mahogany center table with rich satinwood inlay is a good example of how a transitional piece—here from Hepplewhite to Sheraton—can be a highly successful design, almost a style of its own. It is Hepplewhite because of its thin tapered legs and stretchers, but Sheraton in the curves. A remarkably interesting piece.

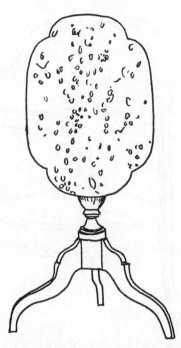

An American tilt-top table with a top of bird's eye maple also has both a Hepplewhite and Sheraton look. Its post is too heavy.

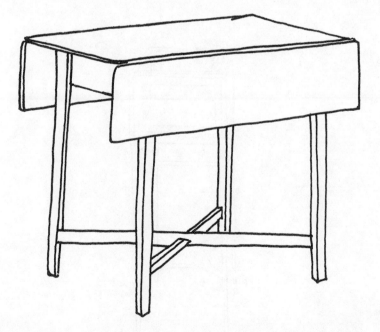

A country-Hepplewhite Pembroke table made in New England circa 1800. The wood is maple, and while the legs are not as tapered as much as they could be, such pieces are highly valued as Americana and for their "primitive charm."

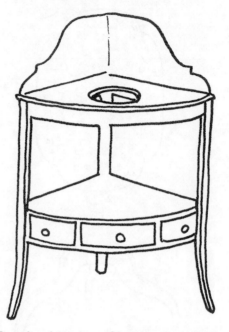

Classical design of Hepplewhite into Sheraton washstand, made in New England around 1810, solid Honduras mahogany. Wash bowl sat in hole on top. Pitcher and bowl sat on bottom over the three drawers used for soap, combs, etc. One in every bedroom of fine homes of the period—early 1800s.

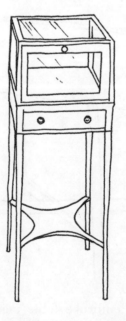

English-made display table with delicate tapered legs of satinwood. Note that the square top retains the Hepplewhite look that was lost in the previous round-topped vitrine.

MISCELLANEOUS

Although this Honduras mahogany bedroom commode has the straight legs of a Chippendale piece, it also has the fine-line satinwood inlay and oval pulls of the Hepplewhite style. And the legs are relatively thin. The slide-out false drawer front contained a thunder mug.

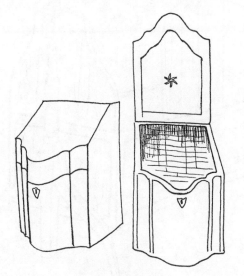

Satinwood inlays, rosewood banding, and curves put this knife box in the Hepplewhite style. The base wood is Honduras mahogany. They were placed on either end of a Hepplewhite sideboard.

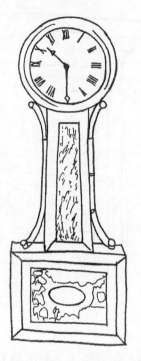

This so-called banjo clock has all the lines and style of Hepplewhite furniture. This one was made in America of figured maple. Reverse painting on glass with clear oval to expose the movement of pendant.

This Hepplewhite swing cradle in cherry was made in America circa 1790 by a country cabinetmaker. Nicely inlaid, but of awkward design.

Typical Hepplewhite mirror frame of mahogany with lots of gilt on decorations. A free-wheeling American piece, could be called "Federal."

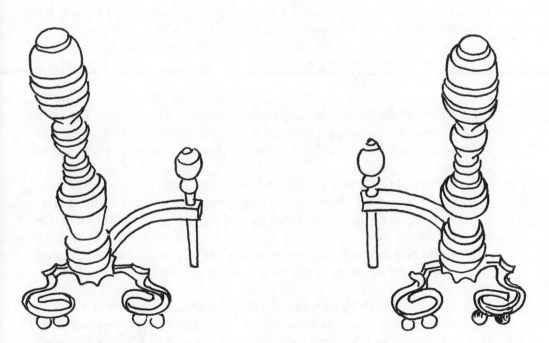

Brass andirons from the late 1700s when Hepplewhite furniture was in style—no particular design connection.

SHERATON, 1790–1830

As in Martha Washington's favorite sewing table

To understand the Sheraton style of the late 1700s, all you have to do is imagine Hepplewhite—the preceding English style—as being made by a Frenchman. For while Thomas Sheraton was undoubtedly English, the style that bears his name came into being as a result of the average Englishman's constant interest in things foreign and especially in things French. Sheraton furniture is simply a modification of the Hepplewhite style to cater to this taste.

In these last years of the 1700s and the first two decades of the 1800s, the French, under Napoleon, had created the new Empire style based on French designers' interpretation of the classical designs of Greece and Rome—an interest aroused by archaeological excavations going on at that time.

So if you apply Empire to the straight-lined Hepplewhite, as Sheraton did, what you get are chair legs that are still thin and tapered, but also round and reeded—this round and reeded leg being the hallmark of the Sheraton style.

And you also get more curved arms and legs—but an abandonment of the shield backs in favor of the more stately square back of the Empire style.

In spite of the unpleasantness of 1776, this style flowed from England to the new United States as smoothly as if nothing had ever happened. In fact it became the preferred furniture of George and Martha Washington, who liked her Sheraton sewing table so much that it is now known by her name.

CLOCKS

A pillar and scroll mantel clock made by Terry in Connecticut around 1830 epitomizes the curves of the English Sheraton style. Figured mahogany veneer on pine, posts often darkly stained maple.

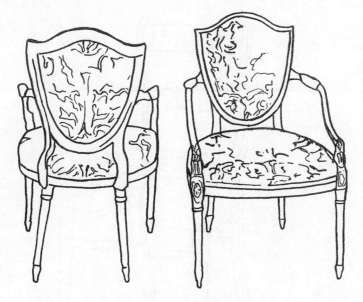

CHAIRS

The shield shape of the backs of these upholstered side chairs may be derivative of Hepplewhite, which is only natural, but the curves in the arms and back supports are pure Sheraton—as are the round grooved legs.

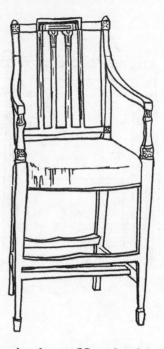

A child's high chair that also has a Hepplewhite look. But curves have come into the arms and stretchers, and the arm supports are turned—a typical blend between the styles of Hepplewhite and Sheraton.

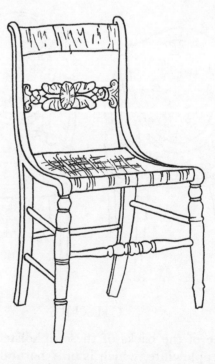

In the 1860s the Sheraton style appeared totally Americanized but still had all the Sheraton curves in the back and seat, the turned legs.

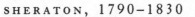

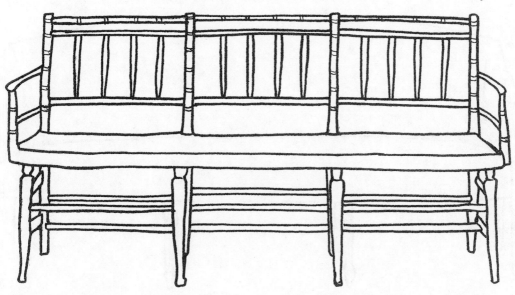

An American variation of Sheraton was the bamboo turnings seen in this "three chairs make a settee" piece. Reed seat, mostly maple, but stained to look like dark mahogany.

Typical upholstered wing chair with block and turn stretcher, round reeded legs, and brass rollers capped on feet.

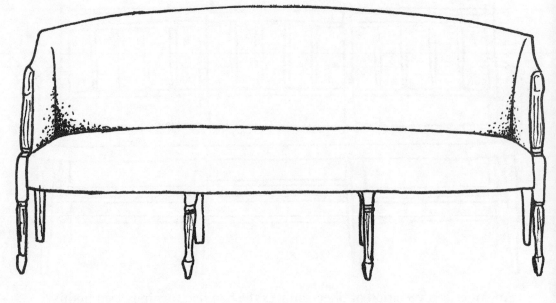

SOFAS

This typically long Sheraton sofa with reeded arms and legs has a graceful simplicity about it and the French touch in the woodwork that makes it unmistakably Sheraton.

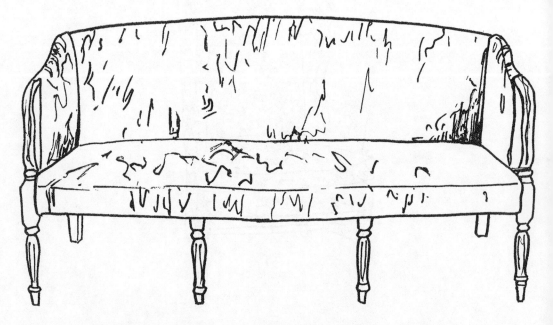

With only minor variations in their long straight backs, Sheraton sofas were the most successful pieces of this style and are still popular.

A small Sheraton sofa with a perfectly straight back looks like Hepplewhite at first glance, but the bolsters and round-reeded legs are certainly
Sheraton.

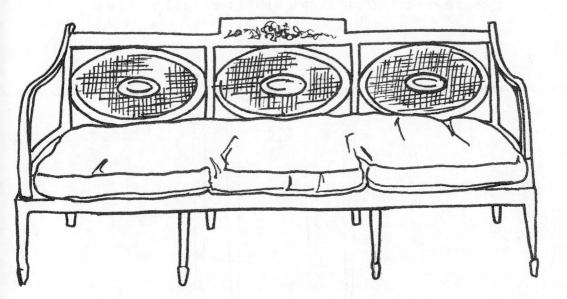

The oval-reeded backs with painted panels give this settee a look that not
only goes back to Hepplewhite, but even to Adam. But the curved arms
and round-reeded legs are certainly Sheraton. Such transitional pieces
are far more common in English-made Sheraton than in the American
pieces, which adhere quite closely to the essence of the style.

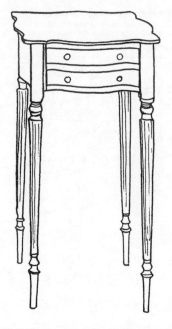

TABLES AND STANDS

Beautifully delicate Sheraton two-drawer stand of Honduras mahogany and satinwood drawers that identify it as having been made in England. A Hepplewhite design now made entirely Sheraton by curves even on the edges of the top—not to mention the round and reeded legs.

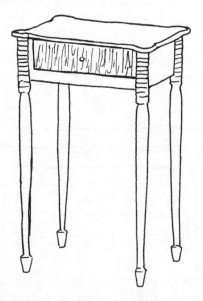

Cookie-cut corners were very popular in American pieces of the Sheraton style. Hard maple legs are not reeded or fluted; the front of the drawer is tiger maple—none of which was stained to look like mahogany.

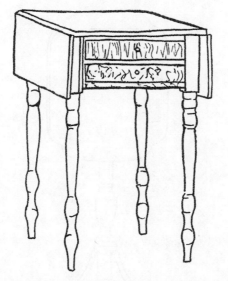

This Pembroke night stand of solid maple and a tiger-maple drawer front was a standard item in the United States during the mid-1800s. In this piece bulbous legs have lost the essence of the Sheraton style, making it more Americana than Sheraton.

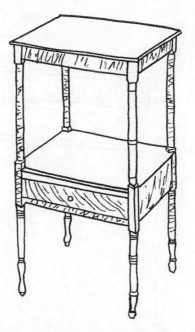

Another piece that would be Hepplewhite if it wasn't for the turned legs and curved drawer front. It is unusual for such a transitional piece to have been made in the United States, but the use of tiger maple does establish that.

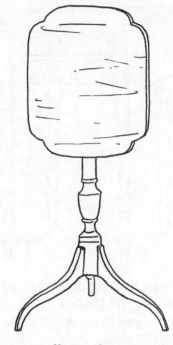

Typical Sheraton tilt-top candlestand: curve-cornered top, urn-shaped
post, double-curve splay lets. Pure Honduras mahogany.

Two-drawer ladies' sewing table with leg tops making cookie corners of
top. Legs not fluted, making this a less desirable English piece—which
Honduras mahogany indicates it is.

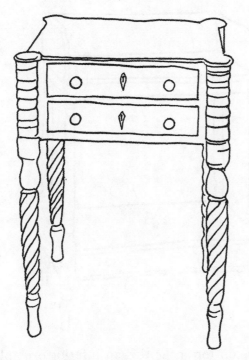

Although cookie corners and rope-carved legs are desirable features, the coarse proportions of this table make it an undesirable piece; it is too heavy.

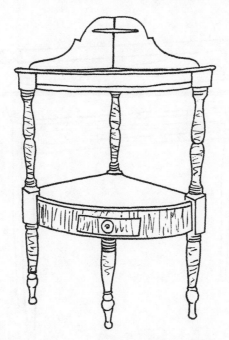

A Sheraton corner washstand with curved back and fluted round legs. Dark red mahogany, hole in top for wash bowl. Bowl and pitcher are stored on the bottom shelf, towels in drawer.

The lack of curves on top make this an inferior example of a Sheraton washstand—but it isn't any other style either.

Sheraton dressing table with rolling-pin back found in the late 1800s. Made of pine that has been false-grained to look like rich red mahogany.

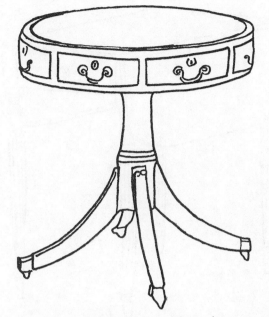

Drum table with typical curved and fluted legs, brass casters, card drawers all the way around; usually had tooled-leather tops. Still being made.

This high-style Sheraton card table with inlay across the front is all
curves and fluted round legs, the essence of this very French-looking
English style.

Classic Sheraton Pembroke table; another excellent example of the style, made in London circa 1835.

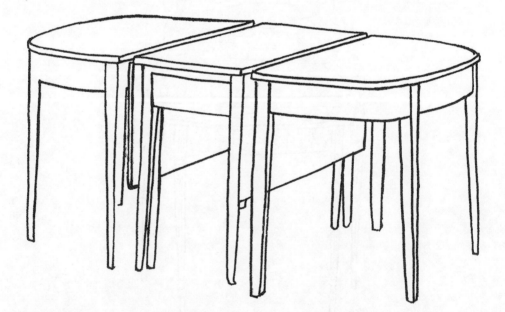

The rounded ends, the heaviness of the legs, and the use of dark red Honduras mahogany give this table its claim to the Sheraton, though the legs make it clearly transitional from Hepplewhite. Nevertheless these assembly pieces are usually called Sheraton banquet tables.

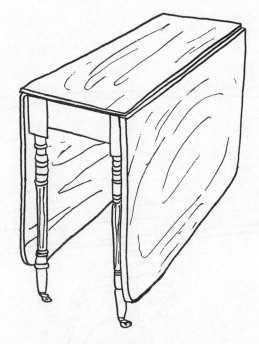

Of course the turned and reeded legs with brass casters are typically
Sheraton in this piece. But the very wide Honduras mahogany table
leaves are also a feature of this period.

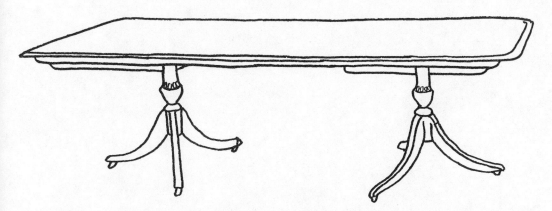

With the use of an extra leaf, two Sheraton tripod breakfast tables are
here joined to make a typically large Sheraton dining table, a popular
piece with the dinner-party set.

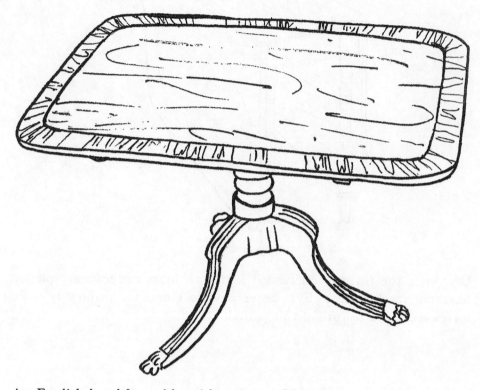

An English breakfast table with satinwood banding around the edge of the top is a masterpiece of the Sheraton era. The tripod base with channeled down-curved legs are a Sheraton signature. There are also brass paw feet covering casters.

CASEPIECES

A fine Sheraton secretary that is the epitome of the style. And of course it looks like Empire, because that is what it was supposed to do. But withall it is a heavy-looking unsuccessful piece.

A successful bow-front bureau with a deck of two drawers on top. Rope-carved outside legs are excellent under cookie corners. Excellent Sheraton.

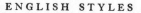

Excellent Sheraton sideboard with brass coasters on fluted legs, fine-figured Honduras mahogany. Such small-sized sideboards are preferred.

Brass rail for hanging linen really makes this Sheraton sideboard with Hepplewhite inlays on doors and drawer. Another typical transitional piece.

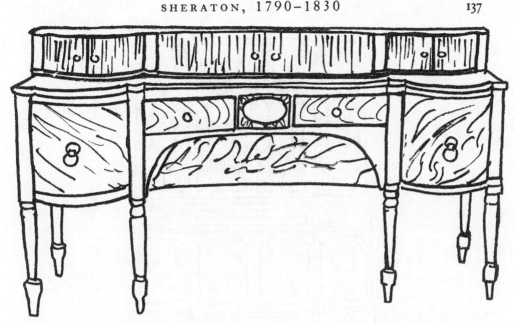

Magnificent Sheraton sideboard made for a manor house in Scotland with tamboured deck across the back of the top. Lines of front and legs are transitional toward Regency, the English version of Napoleon's Empire style.

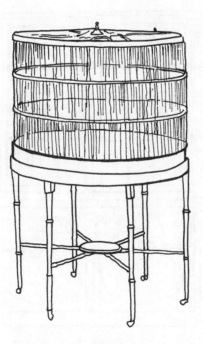

A highly sought brass bird cage on a Sheraton base with delicate mahogany legs and an unusual system of stretchers.

Early Sheraton breakfront with center drawer serving as a small desk. The base has the slightly architectural look of the Adam-Hepplewhite styles from which Sheraton was derived.

A spectacular Sheraton breakfront with a built-in center desk. Oval panels and drawer pulls show Sheraton's roots in Hepplewhite.

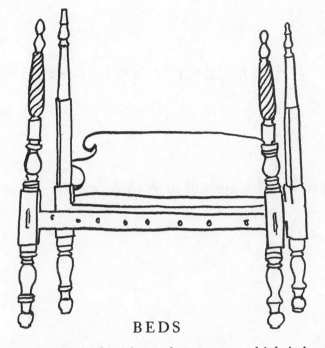

BEDS

Typical Sheraton tester bed without the canopy, which is how they are currently usually used. Rope carving on the posts seems heavy. Holes in the frame were for ropes that originally supported the mattress.

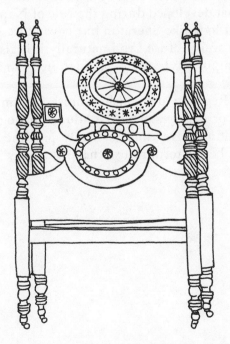

A Sheraton tester bed with bell-topped posts made in England, by a Spanish cabinetmaker using a great deal of Spanish-style inlays in foot and head boards.

REGENCY, 1790–1825

The English version of Napoleon's Empire style

Regency is an indefinite style because it is really only an increased "Frenchification" of Sheraton—already a French-inspired modification of Hepplewhite—that developed during the rule of Napoleon. The result is a lot of pieces that look like Sheraton but have more gilded decoration drawn from Roman architecture. And naturally it is also easy to mistake Regency for the Empire style, then popular in France, that it was so sincerely imitating.

Characteristic of Regency are polished brass moldings and fences on gleaming rosewood or darkly stained Honduras mahogany.

Since the style didn't have time to firmly jell, the term "Sheraton-Regency" is often a better term to use than "Regency" by itself.

This marble-topped table supported by gilded bronze caryatids is a good example of how much an English-made piece can look like Napoleon's Empire style. The use of female figures as supporting columns is an idea taken directly from Greek architecture.

In contrast to the caryatid table, this Regency chair has barely moved out of the Sheraton style save for a little extra flourish in the arms.

A good compromise between the Sheraton and Empire styles is achieved in this Regency breakfast table with its scrolled base and unusual three-sided supporting column. Deeply stained mahogany with gilded molding around the bottom of the column.

An English drum table with alternate false drawer fronts. Gold-tooled dark leather top for playing cards. Bright brass knobs and paw feet. "Sheraton-Regency" is the best term to use to describe it.

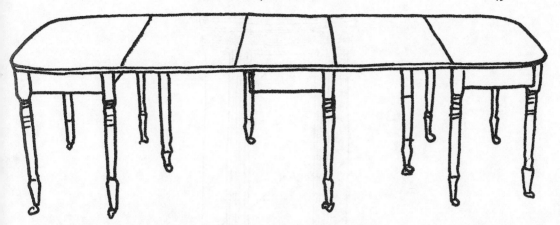

What would ordinarily be called a Sheraton banquet table here slips into the Regency classification because of the brass sleeves over the bottoms of the legs. Perhaps this would be a good time to use the obscure term "Late George III" and walk on by.

A secretary-bookcase with the drawer falling forward to make a desk, which has the elusive Sheraton-into-Empire look that we call Regency. Gilded decorations on deeply stained mahogany.

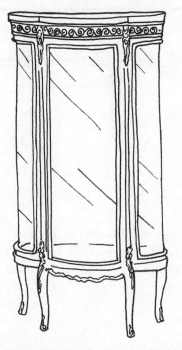

A china cabinet—or *vitrine*, as the French call these pieces—with gilded
decoration around the top and gilded ormolu on the knees of Louis XV
legs. An Empire-looking case on Louis XV legs and made in England, it
all adds up to an authentic Regency omelette.

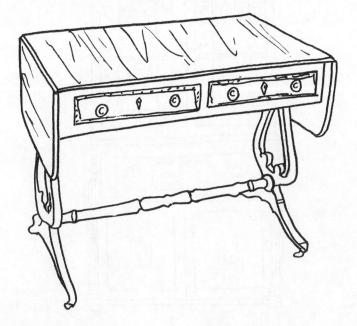

A sofa table with trestle base. The turned stretcher and lyre supports are
certainly of Sheraton, but the brass moulding delineation of the drawers
and knob make this definitely a Regency piece.

A fine Regency breakfront with Empire look in the bare panels of the doors and their gilded rosettes, Hepplewhite-into-Sheraton glass doors above, and a Queen Anne arch on top. A variable English style called Regency.

With brass pulls and feet, and a superstructure for mirror and candles, this Sheraton sideboard becomes a Regency piece.

French Styles

A tale of two cities—the relationship between French and English furniture styles

Yes, the story of the great furniture styles of the eighteenth century is surely as much a tale of two cities as the one that Dickens told. And it reflects just as accurately the economic and political turmoil of those exciting times.

In France it was the furniture of three kings, a revolution, and an emperor. And each style represents a difference in how man thought about himself and how he should be presented on the stage of life. Furniture as scenery—chosen by the actors themselves!

The difference between the furniture styles produced by the two city-states of London and Paris—each at the heart of its own network of colonies—was always clear. The basic English taste was always for straight lines and at its best, a serene austerity. The French taste was for curves, decoration, and applied ornament.

The relationship between the two tastes was consistent. Over and over again the English modified one of their styles by the adoption of what was happening in France at the time. For even then the English considered the French to be more artistic than they and everything French to be more fashionable. This was neatly summed up by Thomas Chippendale himself in 1754 when he published his popular book of design, *The Gentleman and Cabinet Makers Director.* The subtitle was *Furniture in the French Manner.* (See the introduction to the section on Chippendale.)

LOUIS XIV (Baroque), 1645–1705

A decorative orgy that celebrated Europe's rebirth
after the Dark Ages

The style of Louis XIV was the furniture of the Renaissance in full bloom. It celebrated the intellectual and spiritual renewal that laid the necessary foundation for the mercantile expansion of the eighteenth century, the period with which we are mainly concerned.

As such, this furniture was still the stuff of castles, rectories, churches, and monasteries. But since it best reflected its time, we have for it the term "baroque," a word that means florid, bold, exaggerated, irregular, virile, and blustering—if you look it up in enough dictionaries. All of these words express the experience of the Renaissance as well as its furniture.

From the practical point of view, the only authentic pieces of Louis XIV furniture still existing are in museums and state-owned castles. Nor has it ever been seriously reproduced. Its visual extremity and massive size seem never to have captured anyone's fancy since the Renaissance.

Therefore we have in this section only a few drawings of this style in order to respectfully establish the ancestry of the great furniture styles of the eighteenth century.

There is one especially interesting thing about King Louis XIV. He knew exactly who he was and the position he held in history. He called himself "the Sun King" and adopted the sun as his royal symbol.

The style of Louis XIV was a happy explosion of floral and architectural decoration that celebrated the Renaissance, Europe's "rebirth" after the religious sobriety of the Dark Ages—as in this dining table made for Louis XIV by craftsmen imported from Italy, where the style originated.

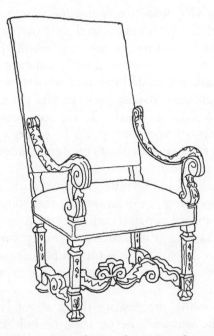

Everything was massive, even chairs, because there wasn't an unimportant piece of Louis XIV—it was all made for castles. That's why you don't find it on the market—all of it that has been discovered went right into museums.

Cross-stretcher table in the flamboyant style of Louis XIV that is usually called baroque. Too important for people who aren't kings to live with, its exuberance was fertile ground for the graceful style of Louis XV to emerge.

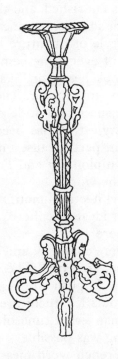

Candlestand for the giant kind of candle used in a castle—and you've gone berserk over the possibilities of decorating things?

LOUIS XV (ROCOCO), 1723–74

Chairs that look as if they might jump in the air

If the reign of Louis XIV brought France out of the Dark Ages, under Louis XV France came into her full glory as a rich mercantile nation with colonies around the world. In Paris as in London, a new middle class of tradesmen and artisans flourished, and they demanded and got a new kind of furniture to express the exuberance of their time.

And what they got was a style of furniture that completely rejected stately straight lines in favor of every line being curved. The idea was that furniture should never look heavy or "just sit there," but should seem to float or be about to jump into the air. And it worked. Beautifully. In fact it produced the most successful style of furniture in Western culture: Louis XV, the one style that has become truly international (though certainly this is true in part because until recently French was the international language of diplomacy and French cultural influence was felt in all the capitals of the world).

The style also rejected all architectural motifs when it came to decoration. Pastoral things were the ideal: shepherd's crooks, shells, flowers, vines, lyres appeared everywhere.

Gilding and bright paints were common, and cast-bronze decorations, which were nailed to the wood, appeared. These are called "appliqués" or "ormolu," and both are now English words.

Perhaps the popularity of Louis XV furniture finally rests on the fact that it was a celebration of man—at a time of prosperity and rebirth when it seemed that everything was possible.

"Rococo" was originally a French word meaning rocks and shells. It now simply means florid or ornate, but it is especially characterized by shell and scroll work.

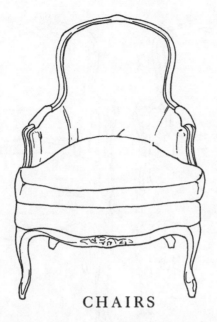

CHAIRS

There is no better-known furniture design than that of this simple Louis XV chair in polished walnut. All of its lines are curves, and all of its curves are in harmonious proportion. When the space under the arms of a chair is closed, it is called *bergère* . . .

. . . as opposed to an open-armed chair, which is called *fauteuil*. This chair is also more typically painted white with gold leaf purposely showing through the protruding surfaces. Often specks of vermillion show through the fine cracks of the gold leaf. Rich.

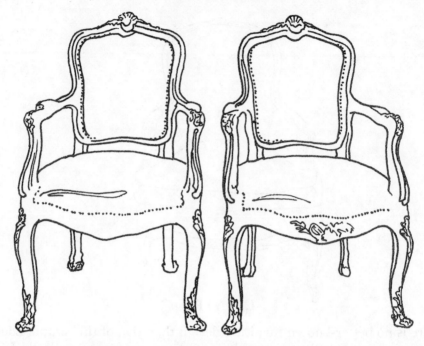

From late in the period are this pair of ebonized Louis XV chairs with applied gilded brass castings on the feet, apron, and crest of the back. Both the ebonizing and ormolu are forerunners of the Louis XVI, Directoire, and Empire styles to follow.

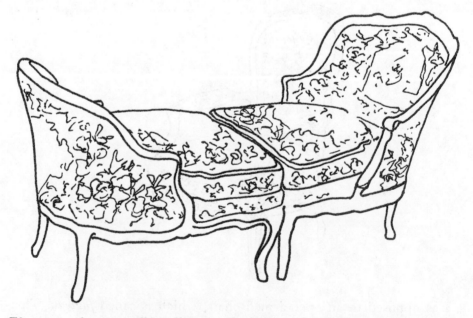

Elegance, charm, and intelligence flow from the design of this two-part chaise-lounge that is typically covered with needlepoint. The wood is polished French walnut, which is much lighter than American walnut.

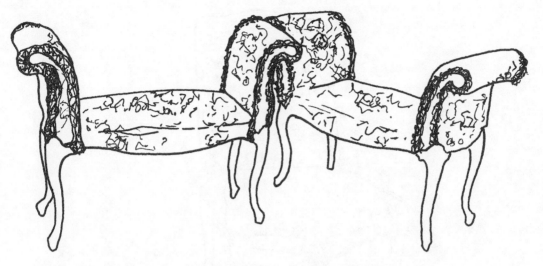

A pair of gazelle-like window benches of the kind that are popular in England. Like Chippendale—its rival for top popularity—Louis XV is still being made in all the major cities of the world.

A piece like this is usually called a love seat, but it is more accurately called a *tête-à-tête* since it is French. This design was popular during the Victorian revival of Louis XV in the United States.

A transitional armchair with Louis XV legs and curved arms, but straight lines of Louis XVI on the sides of the seat and back and an interesting cross-stretcher to brace the legs—an innovation that never found its time.

A pure Louis XV *prie-dieu* made of carved and gilded walnut with well-padded knee and arm rests for long hours spent in prayer. This example is unusually glamorous for such pieces.

TABLES

Classic example of a Louis XV center table with an inlaid chessboard and fine satinwood inlays and gilded brass ormolu decoration mounted on the knees of the legs. All lines are curved except the chessboard.

The amount of decoration places this center table at the end of the Louis XV period, transitional to Louis XVI. In addition to the tacked-on gilded brass ormolu decorations, the ebonized walnut is inlaid with tortoise shell and thin strips of brass called *boulle*.

A copper-lined Louis XV planter made in France during the Victorian era, with the heavy legs popular during that period. It is made of ebonized poplar with applied ormolu and *boulle* inlay. Such reproductions were just as popular in Victorian France as Chippendale reproductions were popular in Victorian England.

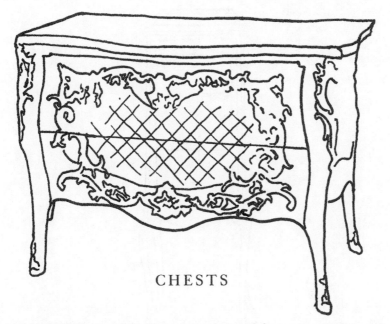

CHESTS

Getting rid of all the straight lines in a chest of drawers was no mean feat for the cabinetmakers of the Louis XV period. But his *bombé*-front commode is a good example of how they did it. This chest has two deep drawers. Inlaid kingwood and rosewood.

Some Louis XV chests had swing-out doors that concealed square drawers inside with lid tops. This one is painted white with gold leaf showing through on the edges of the top and has carving on the legs. Hand-painted decoration in the Italian manner was popular.

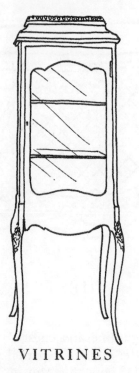

VITRINES

Vitrines, or glass-paneled display cabinets, usually for the storage and display of china, came onto the scene under Louis XV with a new technology that made wide and curved sheets of glass possible.

Vitrine, or china cabinet, from the Louis XV period with decorated panels and ormolu. Excellent proportions! As opposed to . . .

. . . an overweight and clumsy design with especially incongruous rear legs—just to demonstrate that it is possible to go wrong even in the exquisite style of Louis XV.

In this Louis XV vitrine there are as many curved lines as possible without the idea becoming ridiculous—they stopped when it came to the verticals on vitrines. Typical panels on the bottom depict ladies in sylvan scenes.

WRITING TABLES

It must have something to do with the difference between English and
French thinking that the English developed their slant-front desks from
chests of drawers, but the French widened their tables and settled for
two drawers. Certainly the French approach under Louis XV is wonderfully more graceful as seen in this *bureau plat*, or writing table.

Not infrequently a Louis XV *bureau plat* would have a dark marble top to
match its ebonized walnut and applied ormolu decorations.

With drawers and storage cabinets fastened on top of a *bureau plat*, we have a *bonheur du jour*, or lady's dressing table—this one adorned with paintings of cupids and the usual ormolu.

While the legs of this superior writing desk are certainly of the curvaceous Louis XV style, the architectural nature of the top makes this one of the many transitional pieces moving toward Louis XVI.

PIANOS

The Louis XV idea of using as many curves as possible proved very useful in lightening the necessary bulk of a grand piano, and so has been used ever since. Here is an eminently successful example.

Even this pretentiously ornamented grand piano is successful in the style of Louis XV. The ornaments, of course, are gold-plated or -leafed pieces of cast brass or bronze applied with hidden pins that were angled in for greater security.

Most American piano makers have long been famous for their absolute bad taste. In this example of their work, we have Louis XV legs supporting a Sheraton case with typical Sheraton curves in the music holder and pedal support.

In this disaster we have a Louis XV corner leg on the side of the piano case, a Sheraton pedal support, and mediocre everything else.

MISCELLANEOUS

A gold-leafed settee in the Louis XV manner that strongly suggests the Art Nouveau style of the early 1920s, when it was believed that furniture ought to imitate nature by looking as if it was made of growing vines. This piece certainly does.

A chest of drawers in which the Louis XV succeeds in destroying all straight lines except the back of the top.

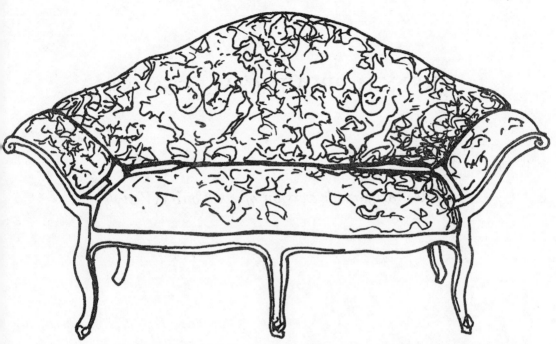

A little upholstered settee in dark walnut and brocaded tapestry that looks as if it might jump off of the floor. Usually found in a lady's bed-room.

A Louis XV commode with drawers for toiletries. Commodes are now more commonly used as small sideboards or servers. Much satinwood inlay and marquetry.

FRENCH PROVINCIAL, 1750–1800

The country-made version of the Louis XV style

French Provincial, or in French usage Provençal, furniture is merely a simplified version of the style of Louis XV that was made in the provincial cities of France in sincere imitation of the richer version that was being made in Paris at the same time.

As such it is the perfect choice for decorating a sunny villa nestled in the vineyards of southern France for one of the Rothschilds. In other words, it is often the choice for casual furniture among the refined as well as the rich. It is the same kind of understatement as is driving a Bently instead of a Rolls.

While the curves of Louis XV were sincerely imitated in these pieces, the country cabinetmakers who made them did use more straight vertical lines. But this modification works well. And of course these Provincial pieces have no inlay work or applied ormolu, which allows them to have a "charming" simplicity. Free of decoration, the lines of the Louis XV idea make their own valid statement.

The usual wood for these pieces is the pale French walnut and the surface is usually only waxed. Fruitwoods, notably pear, were also used.

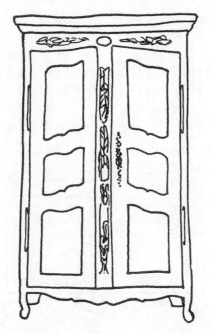

Commonest of all French Provincial pieces is the armoire, a bedroom piece that is often six to seven feet tall. It was used for hanging and storing clothing and bedding.

Some Provincial pieces were more finely executed than others—such as this varnished cupboard of beautifully figured walnut that was originally used in a dining hall of a French country house.

Much of the charm of the Provincial style lies in the beauty of the pale, streaked richness of French walnut and the fruitwoods such as apple and pear that the country cabinetmakers used. No stain was used and wax was usually used as a finish, under which the wood quickly develops a soft patina.

A small chest of drawers made of apple and walnut in the manner of Louis XV, without inlays or ormolu.

An unusual armoire that appears to be a missing link between the styles of Louis XV and Art Nouveau, both of which stressed the idea of using lines found in nature. This piece was made in the late 1800s.

A rather ambitious piece for a country cabinetmaker—even a French one —is this *buffet à deux corps* which simply means that it is a buffet made in two pieces like an English highboy. It is definitely a country piece since it is made of pine.

Only semi-Provincial is this polished walnut cupboard that has the simplified carving of the Provincial Louis XV. It also has glass doors instead of the more common solid carved ones. Probably made for a rich banker in Rouen, a city not all that far from Paris.

This *armoire* is an overdecorated version of the Provincial style that is deceptively made of simple pine to look like the real thing, but which is actually a Victorian imitation. Many like this were made in France in the Victorian era.

A double-doored armoire in the French Provincial style that is painted dusty Italian green with gilded molding. Feet cut off for leveling. The wood is pine. A "doctored" piece—such paint is unlikely to be original.

LOUIS XVI, 1774–93

Legs that look like Roman columns replace the curves of
Louis XV

The French were always able to switch from one style to another more abruptly than the English, and the change from the all-curves style of Louis XV to the straight lines of Louis XVI is a good example.

What happened to spur the change was the great event of the excavation of the ancient Roman cities of Herculaneum and Pompeii, which in the early 1760s became the main topic of intellectual and artistic interest. Travelers to the sites came back to give lectures and show drawings of the ruins, and many articles and books about them were published.

So without any transitional pieces all the *ébénistes* (cabinetmakers) of Paris rushed to present their clients with chairs and tables that had straight legs which looked like Roman columns.

This straight, fluted leg is the hallmark of Louis XVI. The feet and tops of the legs also have an architectural look—though other curves were not abandoned, just played down. Painted finishes and gilding (which also suggested ancient architecture) were almost universal.

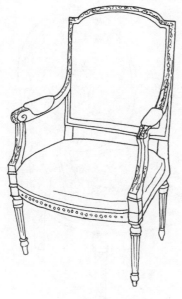

SEATING

In this typical open-armed Louis XVI armchair, the dominating difference from the preceding style of Louis XV is the straight leg—turned
and fluted—with an architectural square at the top. The fluted Roman
columns excavated at Herculaneum were the obvious inspiration for this
leg.

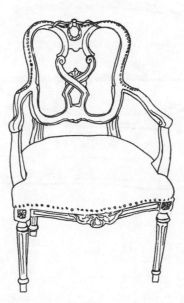

The curved carving in the back of this walnut Louis XVI chair is a not
unusual hangover from the preceding curvaceous style of Louis XV. But
the fluted straight legs with round feet and square tops firmly establish it
as the later style.

A rich round-backed Louis XVI open-armed chair, richly gold-leafed and upholstered with Aubusson tapestry from the French village of that name. The spiral carving on the straight legs is an acceptable variation— simply a device for greater richness.

Salon sets of a settee and two arm chairs are standard stock in the Louis XVI style that is somewhat transitional between the curve-dominated style of Louis XV and the subsequent strongly architectural style that Napoleon would decree for his empire—Empire.

A Victorian version of the Louis XVI style made in the United States around 1880. There is a slightly Eastlake look to this piece—as if that style may have been partially inspired by Louis XVI.

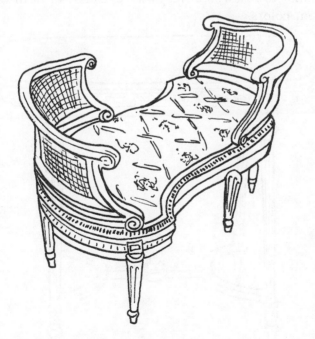

Because it has backs at both ends, this chaise lounge is more exactly called a daybed. Although this is another of the popular Victorian reproductions, the lines of Louis XVI have been faithfully followed, and the use of cane in the backs is also authentic.

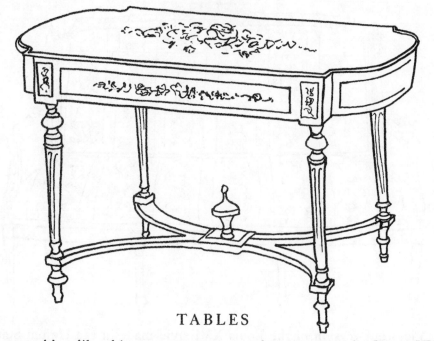

TABLES

Center tables, like this one, are very popular pieces in the Louis XVI style. The most popular wood used was kingwood, a black-streaked dark red wood similar to rosewood. Inlays were usually of satinwood, stained many different colors.

Smaller side tables in the Louis XVI style were often gilded and glazed with chalky paint that was then wiped off the highlights of the carving. Black marble tops are frequent.

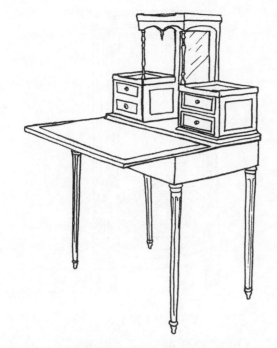

WRITING TABLES

A good example of the style of Louis XVI is this ladies' writing table called by the French a *bonheur du jour*. From the Roman column legs to the architectural top with gilded fences and posts it is truly regal.

Many Louis XVI pieces retain the high-kneed legs of the preceding Louis XV style—or you can call such pieces as this *bureau plat*, or writing table, transitional. What makes it definitely Louis XVI is the gross overdecoration with gilded bronze ormolu on ebonized wood.

VITRINES

A nice example of a Louis XVI vitrine, which has a classical royal look about it. Brass decorations are inlaid into and pinned on streaked dark red kingwood and ebonized walnut. Wood is ebonized by rubbing lamp-black into it and sealing it in with rubbed shellac (French polishing).

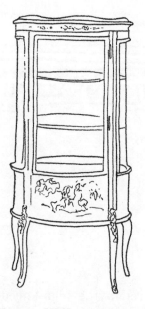

Curved legs make this Louis XVI vitrine transitional from Louis XV. But it has brass decoration on ebonized wood . . . an attractive if indefinite piece.

A Victorian attempt to make a Louis XVI vitrine fails pretty badly in spite of applied gilded brass decoration on ebonized wood.

An example of the American Victorian version of the Louis XVI style. Not an unpleasant piece, but the legs are a total failure—French pig feet.

CHESTS

A marble-topped low chest of drawers or bedroom chest with kingwood drawers and applied ormolu. Bulbous legs seem out of place.

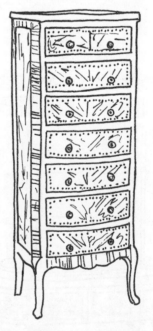

Seven-drawer chest called a *semainier* in French is marquetry veneered with kingwood and satinwood. It has gilded brass decoration. A slight curve in the legs left over from Louis XV is not unusual in the Louis XVI style.

Louis XVI shelf clock in gilded bronze castings and dark green and black marble.

Made in France during the Victorian era—and still being made today— these sets in the style of Louis XVI are made of white marble and gilded brass castings.

Grand piano in kingwood marquetry with tulip and satinwood inlays, applied gilded bronze ormolu.

DIRECTOIRE/CONSULATE, 1795–1804

The furniture of the French revolution, a bridge between Louis XVI curves and Empire's straight lines

The style we call Directoire and/or Consulate is the furniture of the French Revolution, dating only from 1795 to 1804. During the first half of this revolutionary period (1795–99), France was ruled by an elected committee called the Directory (which gives the style its name) and during the second half by Napoleon. The furniture remained the same throughout the period, until Napoleon commissioned the designs that would become the Empire style.

Basically Directoire Consulate style was a more austere version of Louis XVI, based on classical Roman architecture, but often with the addition of revolutionary motifs—the Miss Liberty hat, pikes, stars, arrows, wreaths, and a bound bundle of rods called fasces, a Roman symbol of the power of the state.

The most defined pieces of this brief substyle of Empire (so described because it has many design elements in common with Empire) featured broad black panels of ebonized wood with sparse gilded decoration in the Greek manner using revolutionary symbols. Some of the chairs accidentally came out looking like Sheraton—a French-based English style. A confusing style.

CHAIRS

Excellent Directoire/Consulate chair with a classical Grecian look in the legs and the Sheraton look in the back with its straight top and curved supports. The typical blending of this style.

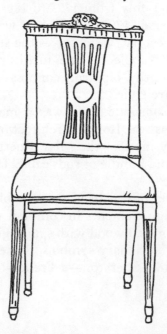

A French walnut sidechair or ballroom chair has the emerging straight lines in the top which would evolve into the Empire style—yet it retains the round legs of the Louis XVI style. The transitional look characteristic of Directoire/Consulate. (Still has the over-all look of Sheraton!)

This chair is in the fully developed Consulate style with heavy gilded brass caryatids. Without them the chair would be definitely Empire just as Napoleon liked it.

French Directoire, which typically blends the curved back and round legs of Louis XVI with the Grecian look of the Empire style to come. Ebonized wood with ormolu mounts and storage space under the seat for cards or papers.

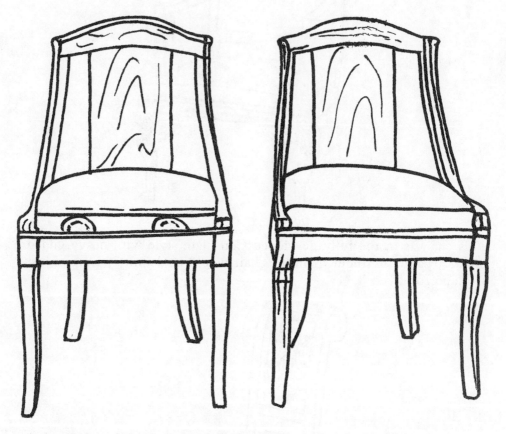

A beautiful pair of chairs in mahogany that are the essence of the Directoire style at its purest—the straight regal lines of Empire with the curved rail that harks back to the curves of Louis XVI.

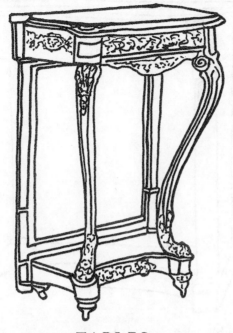

TABLES

Side table or server with the combination of straight and curved lines that characterizes the Consulate/Directoire period. Dark mahogany with ormolu and *boulle*.

A difficult piece—impossible!—to identify in terms of design features, but it was made in the Directoire period and has a Roman wreath and swags.

A simple side table that could be classified as Empire as well as Directoire/Consulate, a common problem with so many pieces of this period.

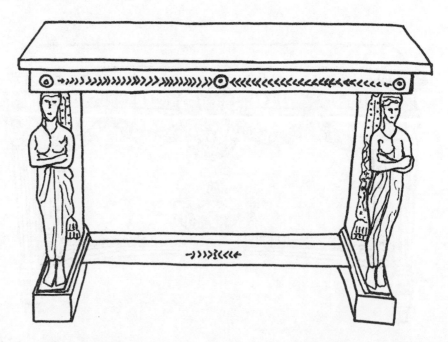

Black marble-topped consul table with mirror underneath; it is classified as Consulate because of the ornamentation and because "it just doesn't look like Empire."

MISCELLANEOUS

A marble-topped bookcase that would be Empire if it wasn't for the curved front supports and ball feet. It is therefore classified as Directoire by default. But then again it could be Regency, the English version of Empire.

Vitrine or china cabinet displaying the restrained curves of Directoire in ebonized wood with slight *boulle* decoration.

Satinwood clock made in France during the Directoire period.

Gilded brass swans adorn this porcelain candlestick in black with gold
stripes from the Directoire period.

An *étagère* made out of rosewood that has the frequent Directoire look of being "not quite Empire." The shelf posts are turned and the legs must have been experimental. Lyrical brass fretwork in doors works superbly, a fine example of the curves of Directoire.

EMPIRE (BIEDERMEIER), 1804–30

The imperial style decreed by Napoleon
based on Roman architecture

Not surprisingly Napoleon knew exactly what he wanted his furniture to look like. He wanted it to look imperial—evocative of the Roman Empire and executed in dark red mahogany with gilded brass ornaments.

So he appointed a committee headed by his favorite furniture designer, one David Roentgen, to come up with a set of designs—which they did, and the style we call Empire sprang fully developed on the scene like Aphrodite from the head of Zeus.

The essence of this style is wide unadorned panels of dark mahogany or ebonized wood, sparsely covered with restrained ormolu of Roman symbols—and after Napoleon had conquered Egypt, with sphinx heads and other Egyptian motifs.

And it worked—to give us the most integrated and therefore the most easily recognizable of all furniture styles, one that is severely beautiful, stately, certainly imperial (even if many of the pieces do look like small black buildings).

From the point of view of design—proportion and line—Biedermeier furniture is the Empire style as produced in Germany, where it caught on and lasted longer than it did it France.

The main difference is that paler woods were used: maple, birch, walnut, and fruit woods. Germany at that time didn't have access to Honduras mahogany the way Paris did, although some mahogany was used.

Biedermeier seems to be the only case we have of a furniture style being moved intact from one country to another—which probably tells us something about the Germans, but I'm not sure what. For whatever it's worth, the name itself came from a cartoon character who epitomized homey, old-fashioned complacency.

TABLES

As Empire as you can get is this console table that looks just the way Napoleon decreed that the furniture of his empire should look—like a Greek or Roman temple with Ionic columns and everything. Lots of gilded carving on richly figured mahogany.

As we all know, Napoleon conquered Egypt to prove that he could do whatever Caesar and Anthony could. As one of the by-products of that conquest we have these gilded Egyptian caryatids supporting the top of a center table. The woods are fruitwood and pale mahogany, which go well with the glitter of the gold.

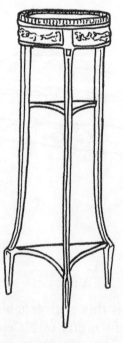

Empire lamp stands were kept light for easy moving and were still made of ebonized poplar and decorated with gilt in the Grecian manner.

A round pedestal table out of Empire that is regressing into the excessive ornateness of the Louis XVI style—almost Baroque . . . but certainly very French. *Sèvres* plaques are set into the top.

An Empire pedestal table with brass rail and applied ormolu on the dark mahogany. But the swelled column reveals it to be a bastardized Victorian reproduction.

DESKS

Looking almost like a Greek temple on legs, this is a typical *bonheur du jour* or Empire writing desk. In all its regal pretention it features *sèvres* plaques, brass railings, applied gilded brass ormolu, and ebonized wood.

A less imposing ladies' *bonheur du jour* featuring mother-of-pearl inlay and gilded brass applied decorations on the ebonized wood so popular in all the later French periods—Louis XVI, Empire, and Directoire/Consulate.

CHESTS

A nice French invention was the gentleman's chest with a drawer for each day of the week, which was therefore called a *semainier* from *semain,* the French word for week. Often they had white marble tops and invariably the gilded brass ormolu and ebonized poplar wood.

A rather ornately decorated commode in the Empire style. Ebonized wood with a white marble top.

The roman fasces—bound rods as a symbol of Roman authority—were favorite decorations of Napoleon's Empire style. Although the feet are a mystery, this lift-top chest well expresses the Roman Empire look so desirable in this French style.

A late Empire side cabinet heavily decorated with *boulle* work, on ebonized poplar. Late Empire pieces—usually more ornate—are often called Second Empire in reference to Napoleon's brief second reign after his escape from Elba.

SEATING

Regal-looking chair of the Empire period heavily decorated with ormolu on ebonized poplar.

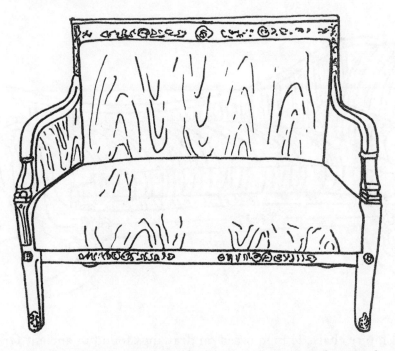

An ormolu-mounted settee in the Empire style is a good example of how the style worked much better with case pieces. The soft curve of the arms destroys the architectural effect stated by the rest of the piece.

This full-length sofa in the Empire style is also a design let down by the arms that are characteristic of this style.

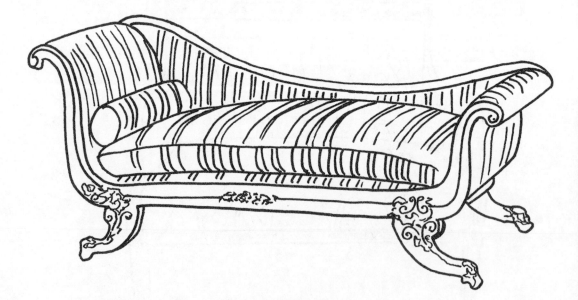

This Empire chaise lounge based on drawings found in ancient Grecian ruins is one of the most popular designs of all French furniture and was avidly picked up by the American cabinetmakers of the Federal period in the United States.

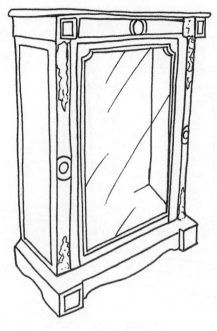

BOOKCASES

A small Empire bookcase with glass door in front has the nice boxy architectural look of a toy building, the usual ebonized and highly polished poplar wood with applied brass decorations.

A *boulle*-inlaid credenza (a form that precedes the sideboard) in ebonized wood with heavy ormolu mounts, a white marble top and glass doors. Late Empire—the more ornamental period of Napoleon's "Second Empire."

An early Empire double bookcase in darkly stained Honduras mahogany is typical of the first designs that were produced to satisfy Napoleon's classical taste. Little ormolu and broad expanses of bare wood.

Late or "Second" Empire double-door bookcase in ebonized poplar with both ormolu and *boulle* of tortoise shell as well as brass. Black marble top.

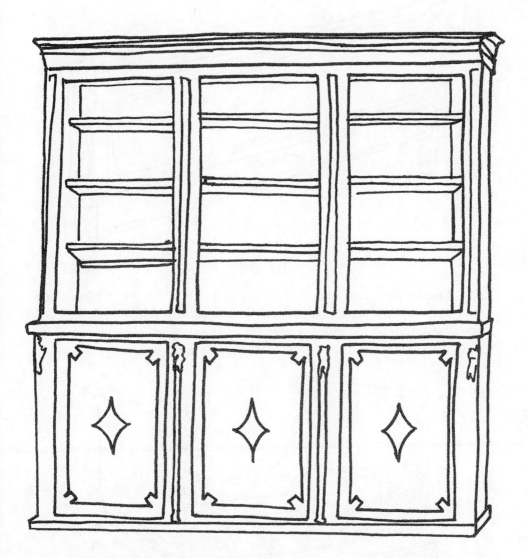

Early Empire breakfront of Honduras mahogany with satinwood veneer on the lower doors and across the pediment. Curved diamond design on doors is unusual—and desirable.

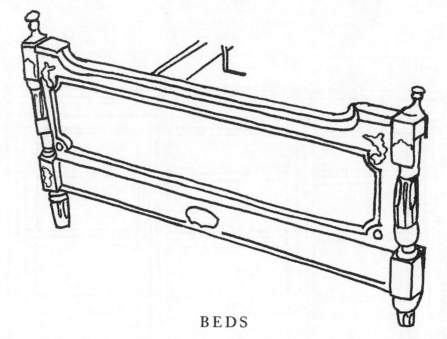

BEDS

Early Empire bed characterized by strict boxy architectural lines and broad empty panel in the footboard, but naturally with applied gilded brass decoration in the Roman manner.

From the end of the Empire period came the famous and ever popular sleigh bed. This serious-looking one is mounted on a separate frame, and the decoration is made of thin strips of brass inlaid into the dark mahogany. These beds are modeled after an ancient Greek couch found in the ruins of Pompeii.

CLOCKS

A typical Empire clock in white marble with an applied gilded base decoration. Such mantel clocks continue to be made in the same manner for export around the world, especially to Texas and Southern California, where the more ornately decorated pieces of the Empire style are popular.

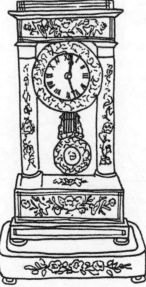

A grand example of clockmaking in the late or Second Empire style. This one, of rosewood inlaid wth satinwood and brass, comes as close as possible to looking like a Roman temple or triumphal arch.

This bracket clock of ebonized wood with restrained ormolu decoration looks distinctly Empire, but it was made in London during the Regency period when the French style was often faithfully copied.

A beautiful bronze casting of a Greek goddess adorns this black mantle clock in the classical Empire style. Authentic though it may seem, it is actually a mass-produced object of the Victorian era. Many such were made.

MISCELLANEOUS

Detail of a screen from the Empire period, which has the ultimate classical touch of a Greek temple pediment at the top. Even in the seventeenth-century, Puritanism was not a French problem.

A Victorian-era piano made in France with the trappings of Empire decoration. Empire was a style that hung on in the popular taste for at least half a century after it reached its peak.

American Styles

We had English styles up to 1776—French ones after that

During the whole of the eighteenth-century, American furniture was a reflection of whatever style was currently popular in Europe—in England up to 1776, and then the styles that were currently popular in France after that. So the pieces based on English styles are called Colonial, and those based on the French styles are called Federal.

The Colonial pieces run the whole gamut of the basic English styles: William and Mary, Queen Anne, Chippendale, Hepplewhite, and Sheraton. The Federal pieces are based on the French styles of Directoire/Consulate and Empire. But Sheraton, the last of the English styles, is also classified as Federal because it was in use during and after the Revolution. (And though English, it *was* inspired by the French style of Empire.)

The American difference in the case of English-style furniture made in Colonial America is most easily seen in the use of native woods such as maple, cherry, and walnut—instead of the ubiquitous Honduras mahogany used in English pieces.

Also in the pieces made in America there was often a simplification of design and ornamentation—especially in Chippendale. For the furniture made in Philadelphia, however, just the opposite happened: there was an overemphasis on decoration—especially in Chippendale.

As for the Federal pieces in the Greco-Roman style of Empire, the most obvious clue to a piece being American would be the decorative use of an American eagle, pineapples, and cornucopias. Pineapples were often brought back from the Pacific by whaling vessels and came to be regarded as symbols of good luck, prosperity, plenty—the same feelings being represented by the cornucopia or "horn of plenty."

The most outstanding furniture of the Federal period was made by a New York City cabinetmaker named Duncan Phyfe, who achieved a fine blending of the Sheraton and Empire styles, usually featuring a lyre, pineapples, and finely carved acanthus leaves.

A third class of American furniture is the country-made or primitive pieces. These are the tables, chairs, and beds made by small-town carpenters in the winter months when the weather was too bad for outside work. But ordinary farmers also made some of their own furniture—especially cobblers' benches, which explains why there are so many of them.

In almost all of these primitive pieces some trace of a recognized style can be found, such as the tapered Hepplewhite leg of a New England night table or an Empire curve in the back of a wash table. In these pieces pine is the dominant wood, because of the ease with which it could be cut and shaped.

Many pine commodes and chests of drawers that are sold as Early American are actually early Victorian cottage furniture sold by mail-order houses. These have been stripped of their paint, chamfered, and stained. They can be easily identified by their paneled sides (as opposed to solid boards) and the machine-cut regularity of the dovetailing of their drawer ends.

COLONIAL (English influence), 1650–1750

Mostly country-made versions of the current English styles

There is no Colonial style, *per se*, of American furniture. The ladies and gentlemen who lived in the British colonies of America were as thoroughly English as their families in England and avidly followed the styles that were popular in London over the years.

These years were from around 1650 to the Revolution of 1776. The styles were all of those listed in the first section of this guide. Some of this furniture was imported from London, but most of it was made by cabinetmakers who had apprenticed in London and then immigrated to Philadelphia, Boston, and New York.

So the differences in design were minor and have been pointed out in American variations included in the section on English styles. These variations are basically the frenetic overdecoration of Philadelphia Chippendale and the conservative restraint exercised in the pieces made North of Boston.

But that still leaves a wealth of country-made pieces that are simplifications of the English styles that were popular in the Colonial cities as the English styles passed through their phases of popularity.

In addition, the American country cabinetmakers developed the ladder-back chair into a style of their own and achieved a triumph with their vastly improved version of the Windsor chair.

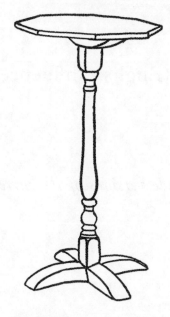

CANDLESTANDS

This earliest type of candlestand certainly relates to the early Jacobean English style in its post turning. But having four feet it must rest on a perfectly flat surface in order not to wobble. However, the Queen Anne, Hepplewhite, and Sheraton (Federal) styles that followed solved that problem. Oak.

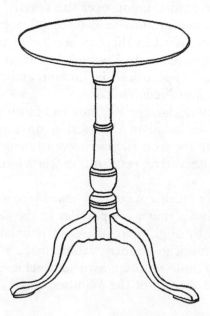

Splay-legged maple candlestand of light maple with clear finish. Thin tapered legs and Grecian vase column are derivative of the English Hepplewhite school.

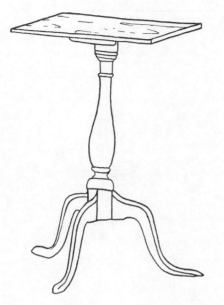

The classic curves of Queen Anne are seen in this swelled-post candle-stand made of maple that can't wobble because it has only three legs. An early demonstration of the principle that less is more. Square tops on Queen Anne candlestands are replacements.

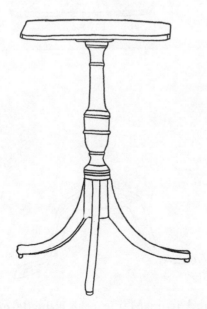

Spider-legged version of the ubiquitous maple candlestand of the pre-Revolutionary era in America.

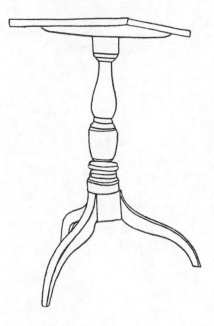

Another Queen Anne table with characteristic double-curve legs and snake feet. New Englanders preferred this serious post to the sensuality of the more classic swelled one. The influence is Greco-Roman—the straight column combined with a vase shape. Maple, clear finish. (Indicates use of shellac—then called "spirit varnish.")

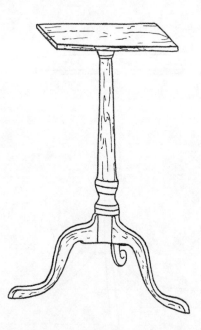

Primitive candlestand from Maine that is made entirely of pine. Thin snakey legs, severe column-on-vase shape, small square top—a true delight for collectors of Americana.

BEDS

Literally millions of four-poster beds were made in the 1700s and 1800s—you almost had to have one to get married. The posts and frame were maple; the headboard was usually pine or cherry. This style of post is called ball and bell.

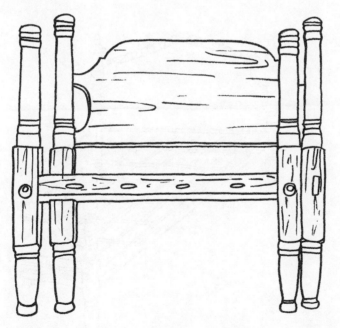

The turnings on no two beds were ever exactly alike, and this bed is included to show just how dull and uninteresting the posts could be. The holes in their frames were strung with rope to make a net that supported a mattress of hay or feathers, depending on your station in life.

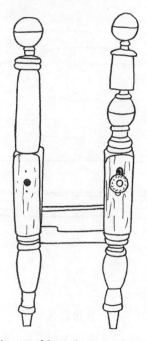

One of the infinite variations of hand-turned cannonball posts from beds made mostly of cherry and maple. The fastening bolt goes into a hole on the left post. Hanging brass escutcheon covers the hole on the right post.

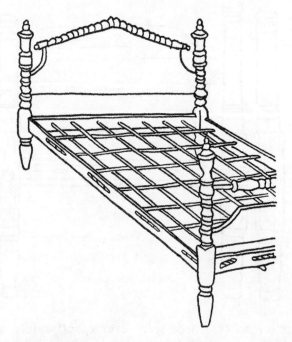

Popular spool bed with rope mattress, from the early 1800s. Later ones with curved-spool turnings come from the Victorian era. Sometimes they were all pine. They usually had maple posts.

A fine example of an American-made Sheraton tester bed made of either cherry or mahogany. The point of these was to keep warm in winter by covering the top and draping the sides to keep drafts out and body heat in.

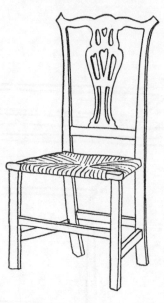

CHAIRS—COUNTRY CLASSICS

"Country Chippendale" chairs were very common during and after the Chippendale period. They were made by country cabinetmakers in imitation of that new-fangled style which the landed gentry had picked up. But the shaping and carving are always noticeably rough on such pieces.

An example of "country Queen Anne," which follows the construction principles of the ladder-backs, but which has a Queen Anne shape instead of the slats. These chairs were, of course, earlier than the country Chippendale, and there are far fewer of them around.

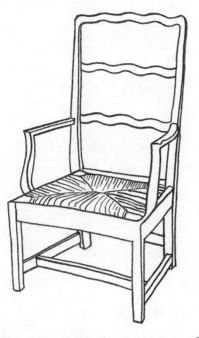

The rush seat identifies this ribbon-back country Chippendale as being American-made by a country cabinetmaker in the early 1800s, though the craftsmanship is much finer than usual.

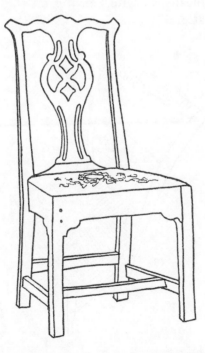

Made entirely of cherry and stained to imitate the Honduras mahogany used by the English cabinetmakers in New York City and Philadelphia, this chair must also be classed as country Chippendale. A coarseness in the carving is always an obvious sign.

CHAIRS—FANCY

Lady's or fancy chairs, a popular peddler's item throughout the 1800s, were mostly based on the Sheraton style as adapted to the machinery of American chair factories. Here is a noticeably Sheraton-looking example, but it also has typically Federal carving on the back slat. A common combination in that era.

The ultimate development of the Sheraton fancy chair sold by peddlers throughout the northeast was the chair made by the Hitchcock chair factory in Connecticut—which is still operating full blast because of the undying popularity of the chair's design and stenciled decoration.

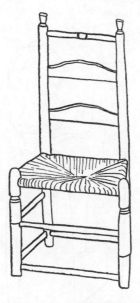

CHAIRS—LADDER-BACK

Early ladder-back chair with only two splats and replacement rush seat. Posts were usually of maple, but any hardwood could be used. Splats are usually of bent ash, hickory, even oak. There is a towel bar across the top.

Three-splat ladder-back with towel bar. The ordinary chair of the Pilgrim era, ladder-backs were commonly used on the dirt floors of log cabins and taverns, which accounts for the rotting of the bottoms of the legs. The legs were then "evened-off."

The most valued aspect of ladder-backs are the turned finials at the top of the back posts; these finials come in an infinite variety.

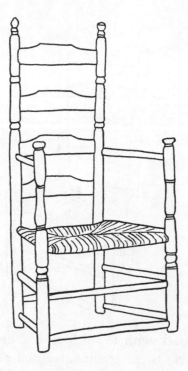

This fine four-slat ladder-back chair of maple and ash is said to have mushroom-top arms. These high front posts are from pre-1700.

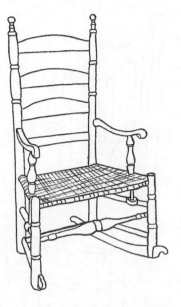

The stepped-back arms of this ladder-back are believed to have been designed to accommodate hooped skirts. Often used as porch furniture, these rockers date from as late as 1850. Called a hoop-skirt rocker, of course.

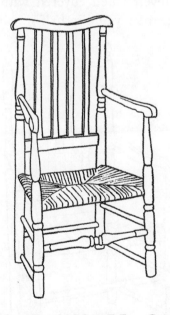

CHAIRS—BANISTER, CARVER

The earliest American chairs were the banister-back chairs, so called because the backs are made of turnings for staircase railings that have been split down the middle so your back can rest against the flat side. Made of all hardwoods, this one has a shallow-yoke top. These chairs originated with the Pilgrims and were made through the early 1700s.

This deep-yoke-backed banister chair has the usual splint seat made of steamed ash strips woven while still wet. Original blood-and-milk paint finishes are treasured even when covered with 250 years of soot and grime. Refinishing cuts their value in half.

Well-designed banister chair with a high-crest back that dates it from as late as 1750. Made almost entirely of curly maple, which makes up for its having been refinished fifty years ago.

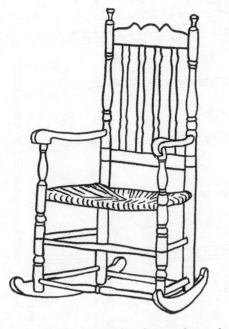

Crested-back banister backs are usually later than the yoke backs, and this one has had rockers added to it for Granny or Aunt Emma, a frequent occurrence, but one that is looked down on by purists.

Chairs made completely of turnings are usually called Carver or Brewster after reputed early makers of them in the 1700s. Very valuable, many fakes. Maple, oak, and cherry turnings.

CHESTS—DRAWERS, LIFT-TOP

Early country-made chest of drawers in the William and Mary manner—note the turned ball or turnip feet, the base molding, and the fake drawer fronts on the top half, which is really a lift-top blanket chest. Most such chests were made in pine and painted with a mixture of blood and milk.

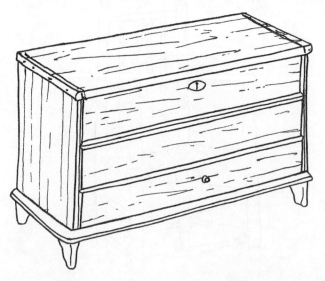

Early low lift-top blanket chest with one working drawer on the bottom. The feet are cut out of the sideboards. The top has breadboard-type braces on its ends. The moldings on the base and front are suggestive of William and Mary. Also made of pine with red-milk paint.

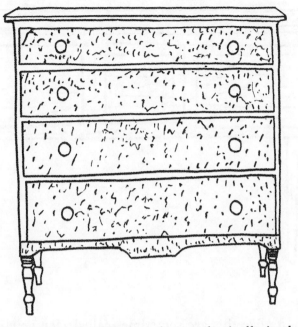

A country-made version of a Sheraton bureau basically in the turned legs and simple round wooden knobs. The country cabinetmakers didn't have access to brass drawer pulls. The graduated drawers and use of curly maple make this a quality piece.

A standard and ubiquitous lift-top blanket chest with two working drawers on the bottom. Since every bedroom needed one to store clothes as well as blankets, they were "mass"-produced in pine and painted dark red—often with streaks of black to vaguely suggest the Honduras mahogany used for the furniture in the great folks' house.

Primitive chests like this are sometimes called Hepplewhite because of the curves in the bracket legs. But primitive American country furniture is what it really is. Most were made of pine with red and black false graining.

A country-made lift-top blanket chest whose painted decoration definitely does make an effort to look like Sheraton in the skirt and painted-on "inlay" striping with cut corners. The finish is false-grained paint over pine.

The only style element in this table-top desk is the vaguely Sheraton-turned legs.

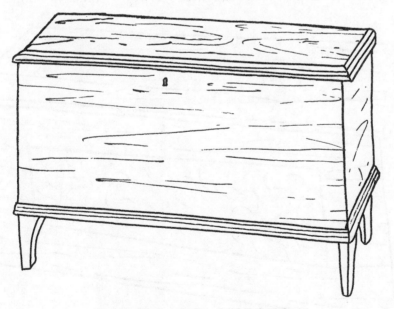

SIX-BOARD CHESTS

This early six-board blanket chest has legs cut from the bottoms of side-boards. The applied molding around the bottom is the design indicator of age. Made of six solid pine boards, of course. In New England, invariably painted dark barn red.

Early Pennsylvania six-board pine blanket chest with false graining and typical hex-sign decoration often on blue- or yellow-base paint. Often made by a father as part of his daughter's dowry—similar to a hope chest.

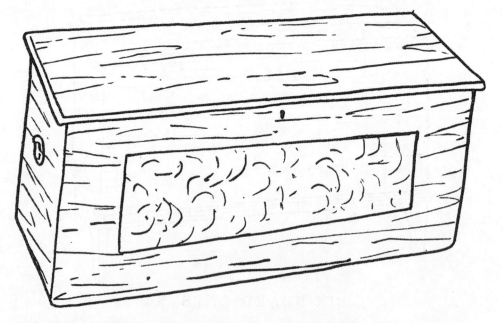

When colonial style six-board chests have metal handles on the ends, they are Victorian; and, if smallish, they were probably sea chests used in the whaling industry. Some were also used for tool boxes by carpenters, etc.

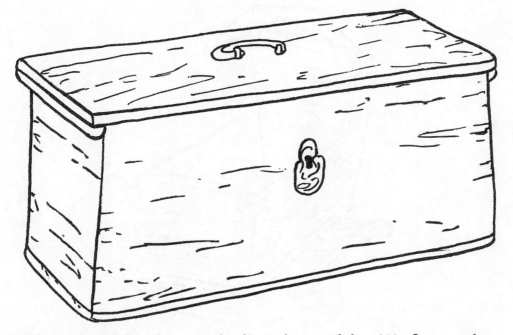

This six-board ditty box was the dispatch case of the 1800s. It was only about fourteen inches long.

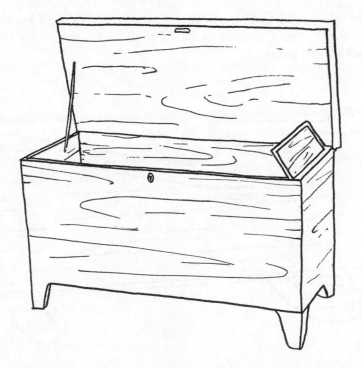

Classic six-board blanket chest with a built-in ditty box, which also has a secret compartment under it. This one is made of poplar and stained to look like mahogany—which by now looks like aged cherry.

CRADLES

Like their cobblers' benches, most farmers also made their own cradles according to whatever designs were locally popular. They were usually low to the floor and had long rockers so the baby couldn't possibly fall out. They were almost always made of pine and were painted and repainted with milk paint.

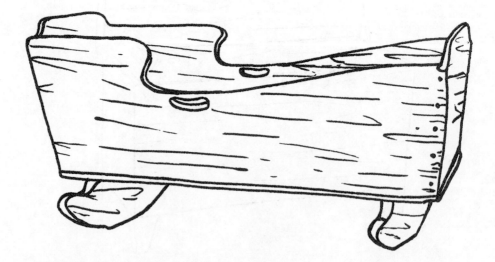

Crudely nailed together, the homemade cradle nevertheless had handle holes whittled out of the sides. The design is a good example of talent coming to the top in primitive works. All pine.

The corner posts used in the construction of this simple box cradle give it an interesting Gothic look. Made of unfinished or "scrubbed" pine.

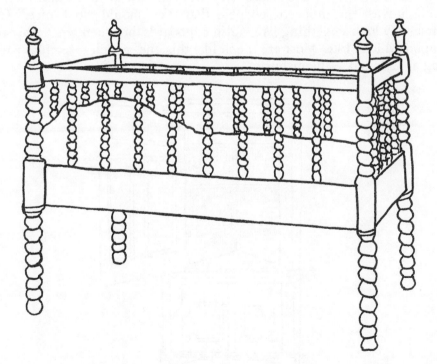

Spool cradles like this one were made by professional cabinetmakers through many time periods. Pine, cherry, maple, and walnut were all commonly used.

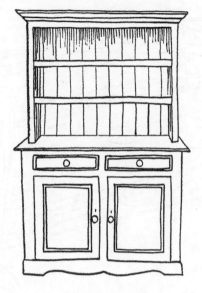

CUPBOARDS

Colonial American cupboards rarely have any identity with the classical English furniture styles—though they do look vaguely English in their solid simplicity. This is because they were almost always built on the premises with the innocent purpose that they should "look nice." Of course they look something like Welsh cupboards, but then what else can a cupboard look like? Most are much like this one, which resembles paneling at Colonial Williamsburg.

Corner cupboards were as popular as the square ones. They were usually made of pine from the local sawmill and were subject to shrinking—thus the use of unattached panels in the frames of the doors.

Yellows and blues were used far more often than reds to paint these homemade corner cupboards, which now all have a lovely patina of sooty grime that drives Americana buffs wild.

A parson's cupboard that may have stood on a table in the front hall of his house—about three feet high. They were undoubtedly originally painted, but virtually all such objects had been scraped and "antiqued" with burnt sienna and raw umber in linseed oil before the current craze for original paint as Americana.

Low wall cupboard whose top could be used as a sideboard or for food preparation. Unpainted pine with outstanding patina, wooden turnbuckles.

One of the most desirable of country-made American cupboards, this style looks like Shaker, but it isn't. It is also much reproduced—always in pine. Made from circa 1750 to the present.

First cousin to a cupboard, this pine dresser was made in the early 1800s. Curves across the top and down the sides were cut out of originally straight boards probably in the 1920s to make it look more "Colonial."

A corner cupboard made in the 1820s or so, with its door or doors removed and the curves cut around the space left to make the piece conform to the then-popular impression of what Colonial should look like. Nice original H-hinges of wrought iron made by the local blacksmith. Pine.

TABLES—SMALL

Typical bedside night table with the tapered legs of the Hepplewhite style. Maple with a natural finish was the most popular wood for these. Some parts were often cherry for contrast.

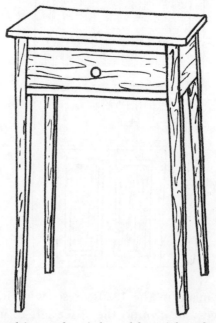

One-drawer Hepplewhite-style night table with splayed legs and top of maple, drawer front of cherry, and a typical small brass knob for the drawer pull.

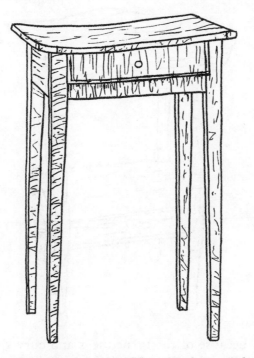

Close to the best of its kind is this Hepplewhite night stand in curly maple made by a highly skilled country cabinetmaker. The drawer is edged in contrasting dark cherry; corners of the top are mildly cookie-cut. Hepplewhite stands are pre-Revolutionary.

The turned legs of this night table indicate it is from the Sheraton period that followed the American popularity of Hepplewhite—say, around 1780. Basically the Sheratons are post-Revolutionary.

Called Sheraton because of the turned legs and curved splash-back, this all-pine washstand was designed to hold a washbowl on top, a water pitcher below, towels on the side stretchers, and soap, combs, and such in the drawer. Made through the late 1800s and sold by mail-order houses.

Perfect proportions make this all-pine night table just as desirable as the solid maple ones, especially with the small brass knob.

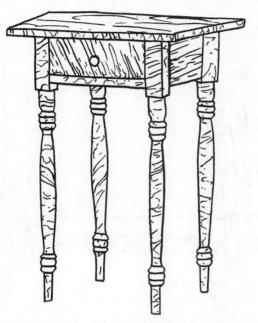

A dazzler among night tables, this one with the Sheraton-style turned legs is made of tiger maple.

TABLES—STRETCHER

Your basic Early American stretcher-base tavern table with a drawer, a well-scrubbed pine top, and turned maple legs. These are quite early and are associated with the William and Mary style, though they persisted in America long after that style had passed in England.

The single stretcher, the bold turning of the maple legs, and the molding on top all give this table a definite William and Mary look. As often happened, the top has been replaced, which accounts for the lack of molding around the edge. But all that needs is a good furniture doctor.

Splay-legged (nontipping) small butterfly table. The name comes from the shape of the wings that support the small leaves. Usually butterfly tables are made entirely of maple, preferably figured, this one is from New England, circa 1740.

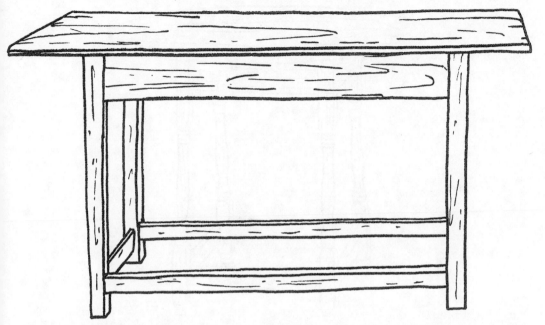

Unusually long stretcher-base table from Virginia, made entirely of hard Southern pine. The top is clean-scrubbed; the base is covered with old dark milk-blood paint.

The widely splayed legs of this stretcher-base writing table are reminiscent of the legs on American Windsor chairs of the period. Fine maple top and single drawer.

Mass-produced (well, relatively) tavern table with an oval top, which was an improvement over the square because it was harder to topple it over during the tippling. Maple base with pine-board top.

Better oval-topped maple tavern table with tiger-maple top, a drawer, and turned legs. This piece was more likely used in a rich man's house than in a tavern.

TABLES—VARIOUS

A very early tavern table with Queen Anne-style arches in the frame and William and Mary button feet. Country-made, of course, a true relic of the early English settlers in New England. Maple legs, walnut skirt, and pine top that is probably a replacement added about a hundred and fifty years ago.

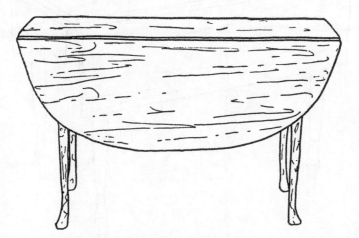

Very early American-made table after the Queen Anne style by a country cabinetmaker outside of Boston. Mostly these were made of cherry, because cherry could be streaked with lamp-black and stained with berry juice to look just like the more valuable Honduras mahogany used in England and Philadelphia by the rich government class.

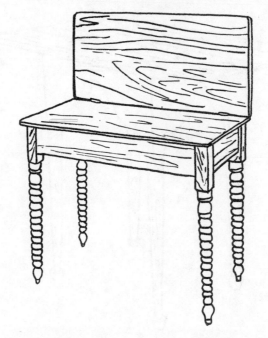

Spool turning was popular to one degree or another from 1700 to 1900. This cherry wood folding-top table with a swing-out rear leg could have been made at any time from 1750 to 1850, and represents no style at all except for the spool legs.

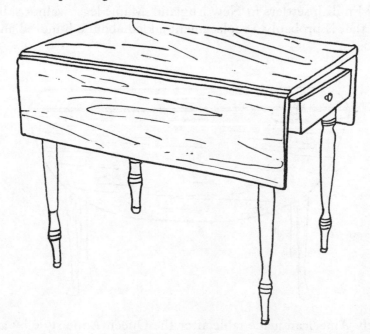

Country-made drop-leaf table with maple legs and pine Pembroke top. No two legs of it are turned exactly alike. With a little effort you could call it country Sheraton, though they are usually sold as "Early American."

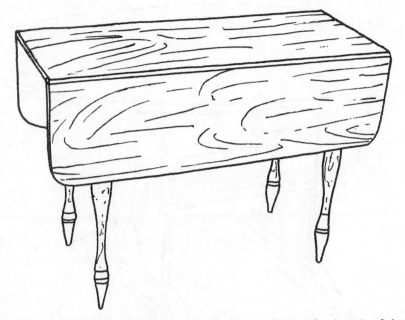

Birch drop-leaf table with lemon-bulb legs, obviously inspired by the Sheraton style of the mid-1700s. Originally stained with berry juice to look a little like mahogany.

Hutch tables were usually made of pine, but sometimes they have maple tops. When opened up, they not only made imposing chairs but had storage spaces under their seats. A basically Dutch idea of no particular style.

When the top of this hutch table tilted back, all you got was a dough box used for kneading bread and leaving it to rise.

Here is a small hutch table with a well-scrubbed breadboard top. The frame was painted with blood-milk paint. No style—just a hutch table. American country.

MISCELLANEOUS

Sheraton tea table with removable tray on top. The wheels were for rolling it in from the kitchen, of course. These pieces were made of cherry, maple, and mahogany. They were madly reproduced during the 1920s by Grand Rapids, but interest soon fell off.

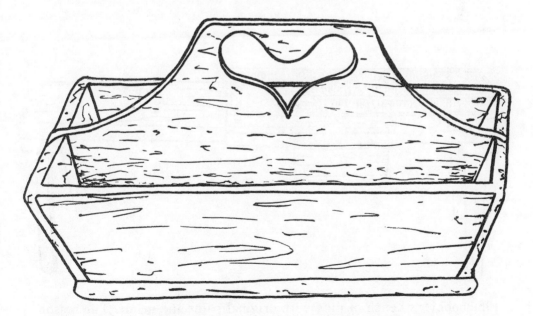

Lovable and quaint knife-and-fork boxes abound, made of pine by Dad on long winter nights.

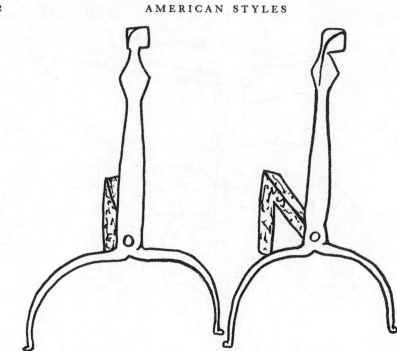

Andirons were made by your local blacksmith; they were his chance to be artistic, so they are real examples of primitive-art Americana. A collector would point out that these have a goose neck, a diamond head, and penny feet.

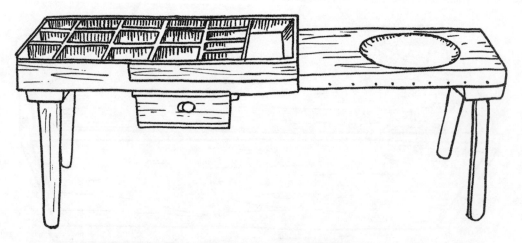

Pine cobbler's bench of pine with original paint and grime. The reason there are so many of these is that most farmers did their own cobbling during the winter months.

A real full-time cobbler used a work table and chest like this one and sat on a low bench next to it. Painted pine, white porcelain knobs.

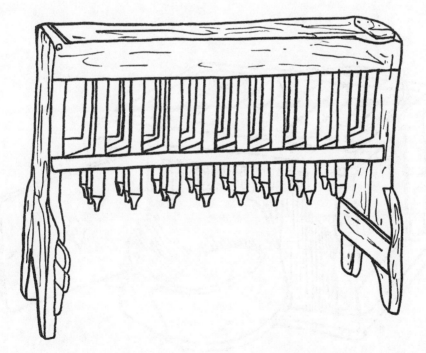

Tin candle molds were first strung with flax thread for wicks, then had wax poured in them. This early one has a wood frame. Circa 1700, this was mass production compared to dipping weighted wicks in hot wax over and over again.

Solid pine doughbox in which bread dough—lots of it—was placed to rise overnight. Many similar ones are now coming down from Canada.

Foot warmer placed under robes in the family carriage or sleigh. Hot coals from the fireplace were put in the tin cup, which was then put in the wooden-framed box of pierced tin.

Ubiquitous spinning wheel made of maple turnings inserted into pine-block base.

This typical pillar-and-scroll clock dates from the second half of the 1700s or Federal era, but it is totally inspired by the Sheraton style of mother England. Mostly mahogany veneer on pine, reverse painting on glass panel in door that opens for lifting weights on the pulleys that made its brass works run. The best were made by Terry in Connecticut.

FEDERAL (French influence), 1770–1830

*A wide variety of pieces derivative of the Empire
and Sheraton styles—but made in the United States*

The term "Federal" is used to describe any furniture made in the United
States in the twenty-five to thirty years after the American Revolution.
And since the French blockade helped us win that war, during the years
that followed everything French was very popular.

There was one exception to the French-influence rule—Sheraton,
which was English and had arrived in the colonies before the Revolution,
was also popular, possibly because it was thought of as having been inspired by the French Empire style. Sheraton, as designed by Albany,
N.Y. cabinetmaker Duncan Phyfe during the years 1790–1820, seemed to
flow together with Empire. Phyfe bridged the gap between the two
styles.

From the simplest Sheraton to the most ornate Empire there is a wide
variety of pieces that somebody is willing to call Federal.

CHAIRS

This Duncan Phyfe chair is a good example of how the very successful New York City cabinetmaker would start with a Sheraton frame and enrich it with Grecian decorations in the manner of the Empire style.

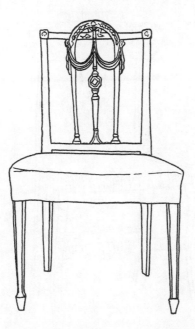

This "New York Sheraton" chair retains the tapered and spade-footed legs of Hepplewhite and has the Grecian decoration of Empire and Directoire/Consulate on the back. It is typical of the Federal period and certainly comes under the umbrella of the Federal style.

New England country chairs like these were basically inspired by city-
Sheraton. But the scrolled arms are out of Empire, and the rush seats and
hand-stenciled decoration are one hundred percent American—which
adds up to country-Federal.

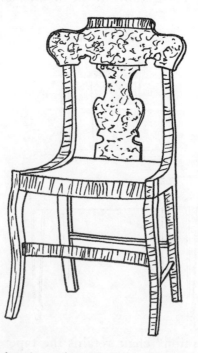

A fiddle-back chair that is as American as the curly and tiger maple it is
made out of. The inspiration behind its curves, however, is out of Empire. Made in 1775—Federal.

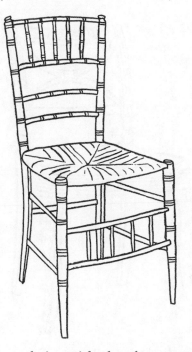

A Sheraton ballroom chair with bamboo turnings and bird-cage stretchers made in the 1790s. A very original American piece of the Federal era.

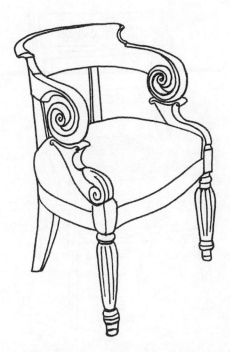

With strangely fat Sheraton legs and the wide curves of Empire on the top, what can this piece be called except Federal?

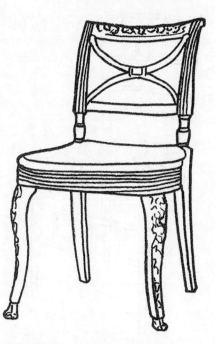

Federal chair that typically blends Sheraton and Empire styles. With the unusual extra touch of Louis XV front legs.

The turnings and squared top rail of this chair are definitely inspired by Empire and the seat and legs by Sheraton, a typical blend of the Federal period in the United States.

A totally American blend of Sheraton style and Windsor construction (posts into thick plank seat) results in a typical Federal fancy chair. Always ornately hand-painted on a green or yellow base.

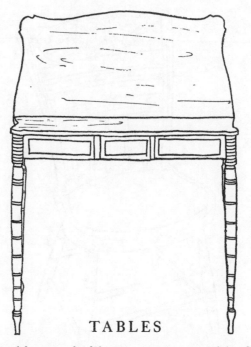

TABLES

A Sheraton card table exactly like one once owned by Martha Washington. It features serpentine edges and American-flavored bamboo turnings on the legs. One of the many varieties of pieces that come under the rubric of Federal.

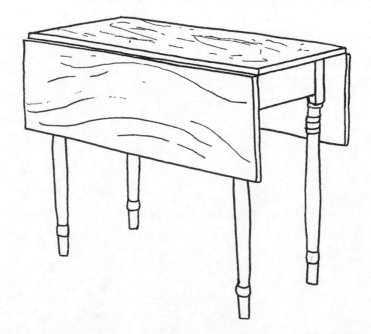

A simple country-made drop-leaf dining table made of cherry in Connecticut, circa 1790. Thus it is American-Sheraton-Federal.

A popular two-drawer night table with the round legs of Sheraton but boxy-looking drawers of Empire, with maple and mahogany veneers on them. Made in the United States after the Revolution.

The rope-carved legs of this two-drawer Sheraton night table are as Federal as you can get.

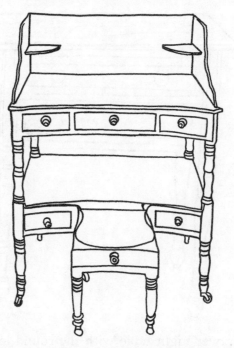

A gentleman's washstand with a pull-out stool has Sheraton legs, Empire drawer fronts, and an American splash-board back.

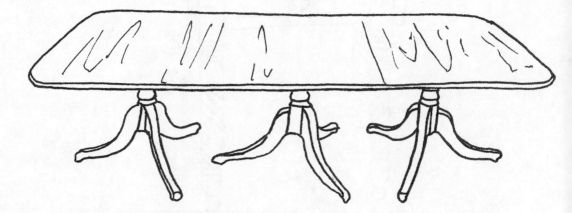

A three-tripod dining table that is definitely Sheraton in the curve of its legs and was very popular in the Federal era.

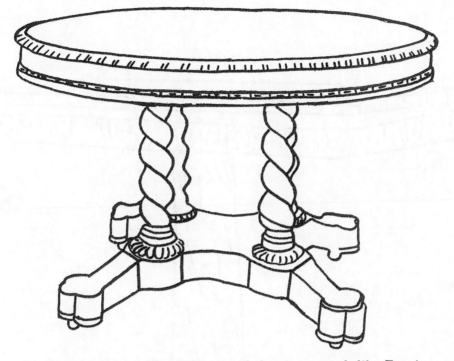

An oval-topped center table with a stand that is as much like Empire as you can get. Made in the United States by a contemporary of Duncan Phyfe and classified as Federal.

An Empire card table in the manner of Duncan Phyfe, typified by the brass inlays into the mahogany, a fussier style of ornamentation than the bold ormolu of genuine Empire.

Pedestal-base card table made in the Federal period after French Empire
style with no ornamentation but quality workmanship with fine figured
mahogany. Precursor of how the Empire style would be treated in the
American Victorian era.

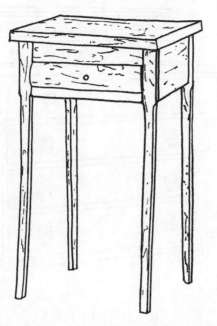

The Federal or post-Revolutionary taste for France's Empire style is seen in this night table—the untapered legs and swelled front drawer were covered with mahogany veneer, and the whole piece was stained dark red. What worked for Hepplewhite is a true disaster when tried in Empire.

Not uncommon were tapered-leg night tables that doubled as washstands with back leaves that folded down in back when not in use. The two turned wooded knobs date this piece to the late Empire period—as opposed to the single small brass knob of the Hepplewhite examples.

CASEPIECES

A perfect example of the use of Empire during the Federal era in the United States, this piece is squared up and has the lines of Greco-Roman architecture—as opposed to the broad curves of the Empire-inspired pieces to come in the Victorian era.

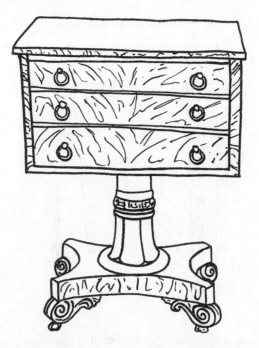

A pedestal-base sewing table in Honduras-mahogany veneer that is very much in the Empire style—though the drawer pulls are a Sheraton touch, and the size of the drawer case is a practical American one.

Federal period American-designed Empire chest featuring the spiral posts popular in the United States and in the Empire classical architectural lines. The round glass or brass drawer knobs are also strictly American and Federal.

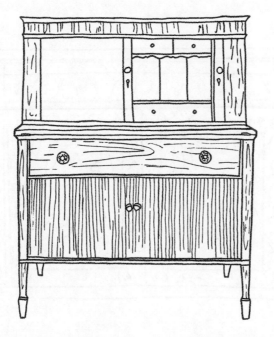

A combination of the Hepplewhite and Empire styles resulted in this tambour (sliding reed mounted on canvas panels) desk made in New England during the Federal era. The sliding reed curtains and square spade-footed legs are straight out of Hepplewhite. But the squareness of the case and architectural top are pure Empire.

Sheraton tambor desk made in Boston circa 1800. Round legs and drawer pulls are the Sheraton modifications of this basic Hepplewhite design.

The Empire sideboard in richly figured mahogany is typically without applied ornament in this American Federal version of the style, though Phyfe did use restrained brass ornamentation in New York City.

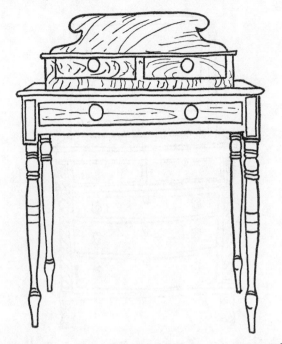

Nice combination of Empire case and Sheraton curves and turned legs in this dressing table that is typically Federal. Some were made of mahogany, some of mahogany-veneered pine, but most in false-grained pine.

Hepplewhite-Sheraton-Empire (drawers-backboard-legs) sideboard in good mahogany. But what an identity problem. Do they have therapists for furniture yet?

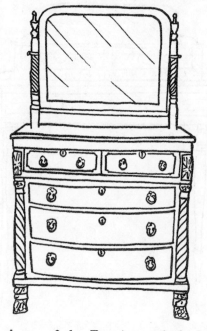

Sometimes the Federal use of the Empire style had all the elements of Empire but put them together in such a way that in the end they looked like old oatmeal—as in this total failure of a dresser made of mahogany veneer on pine.

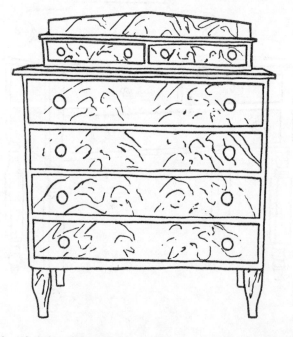

A good example of the "plain" style of Empire made in the United States in the Federal period. Mahogany veneer on pine, no ornamentation. Even the knobs are mahogany.

From late Federal times through the whole Victorian era, these lift-top commodes were America's favorite piece of furniture. Every farmhouse bedroom had one—with clothes in the top, personal items in the drawer, and a "thunder pot" behind the door in the bottom for cold winter nights.

SOFAS AND BEDS

An example of the ornate versions of the Empire style made in New York City during the Federal period. All beautifully carved mahogany, of course. These pieces are best used for decorating museum or movie sets.

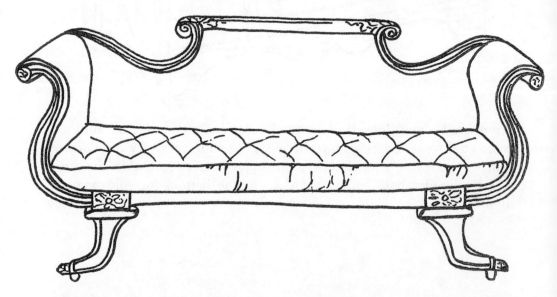

A very restrained use of the Empire style in the manner of Duncan Phyfe, circa 1800. Very Grecian-looking, but dominating and self-important. Basically a failure compared to real Empire and Directoire/Consulate styles.

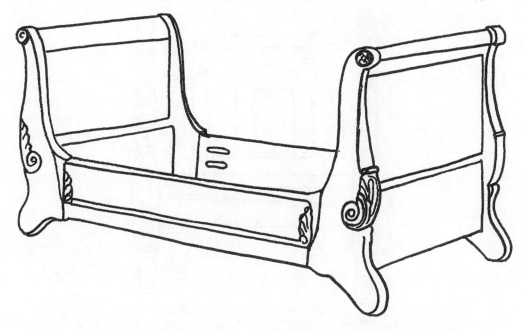

One of the most popular pieces of Federal furniture is this American version of the sleigh bed of Napoleon's Empire style. The lines of classical Greece are still apparent.

Here the regal look of Empire is combined with the round tapered posts of Sheraton to give us an authentic if unattractive piece of Federal furniture.

An Empire four-poster of the American Federal period. These were made of cherry or walnut as substitutes for the far more expensive Honduras mahogany used in France. Pineapple designs on posts and the roll-bar top are very American.

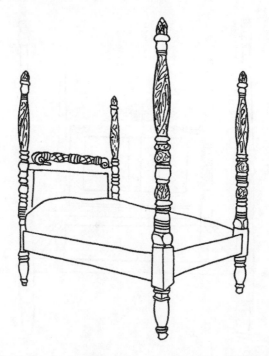

A New York City version of Empire during the Federal period. These were carved out of solid mahogany, but their pretension gives them more historical value than anything else.

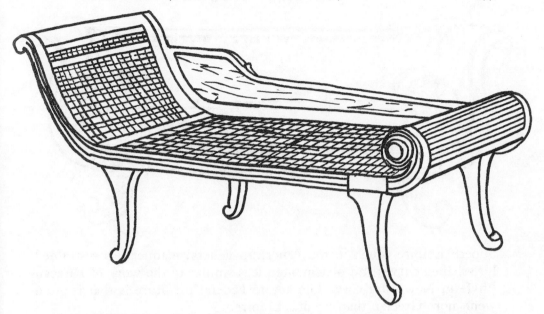

Copy of a Grecian couch was a uniquely American twist to the use of the French Empire style during the Federal period in the United States. Since it isn't really Empire, or really Sheraton, or really anything else . . . it must be Federal.

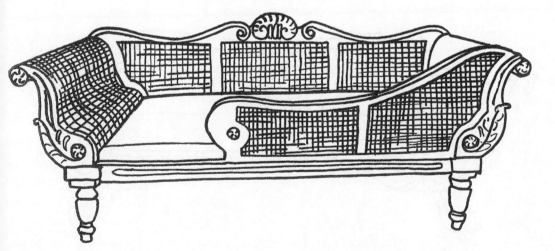

An American-made Empire couch in the unornamented Federal manner becomes a daybed when the front panel is slipped into place to keep you from falling out.

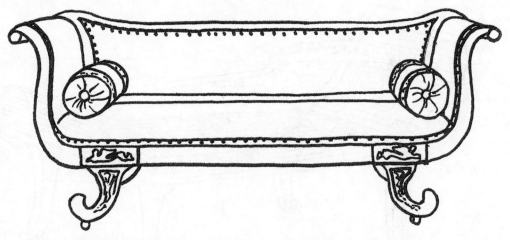

Superb Empire couch in the American Federal manner has restrained lyre-shaped curves and ornamented legs similar to the work of Duncan Phyfe in New York City. The key to Federal furniture is that it often went more Grecian than French Empire.

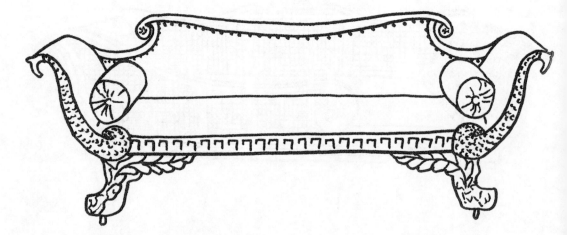

Duncan Phyfe's interpretation of the Empire style has an elegant and regal look with far more gilded ornamentation than the other American-made Empire furniture of the Federal period.

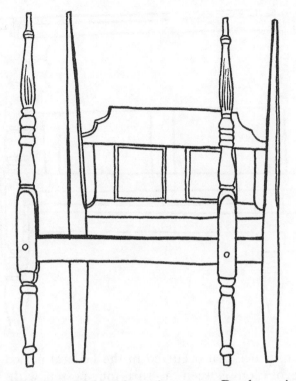

An American Sheraton bed without its tester. Reed carving on the foot posts, octagonal pencil posts on the headboard that look vaguely Hepplewhite and Empire paneling in the headboard. Now *that* is what we call Federal!

Pineapple on bell was a popular post top in first half of the 1800s. As noted earlier, the pineapple became a symbol of happiness and good luck when the whaling fleet began bringing them home from the Pacific islands.

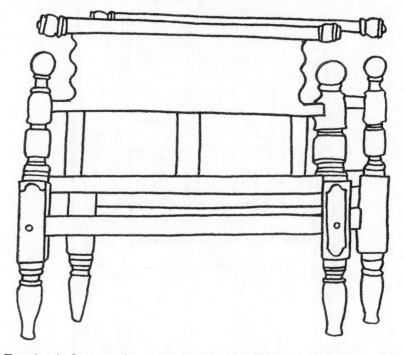

The Empire influence that occurred in the Federal period just after the American Revolution is seen in this four-poster with simple "cannonball" turnings and roll-top foot and headboards. Usually stained or painted to simulate mahogany.

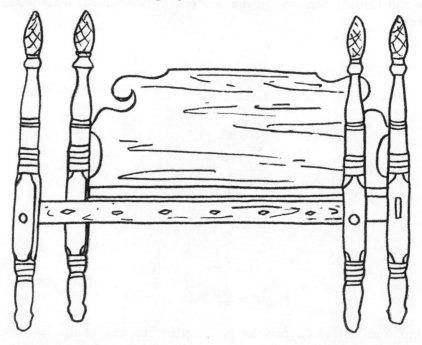

A later bed—circa 1850—this one is made of Caribbean mahogany and features pineapple-topped posts.

MIRRORS

A very Grecian-looking but uniquely American mirror of the Federal period. Frame-gilded, reverse painting on glass in the upper section.

A dumpy-looking Empire-inspired gilded mirror of the Federal period. Its only distinction is that there are thirteen little balls across the top. Thirteen states . . . America's lucky number . . . whatever.

Nothing could be more Federal than a convex or bull's-eye mirror with an angry American eagle astride the top. These were made in France for the American market. They are plaster of paris castings over wood frames, gilded and antiqued with a glaze.

This hall mirror about two feet high can definitely be called Federal because of its exuberant gold finish and thirteen balls under the top. Although stylistically out of Empire, this is a real American celebration.

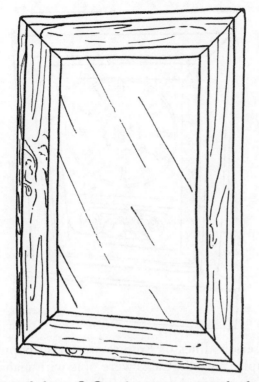

At least a million of these O.G. mirrors were made during the Federal period. Originally made of pine with a fine mahogany veneer, most of them have had the veneer soaked off and are sold as "Early American."

MISCELLANEOUS

Uniquely American are the steeple clocks out of the Empire influence. Also pine cases with mahogany or rosewood veneers.

The square and serious lines of Empire were also popular during and well after the Empire periods. Cases were pine with mahogany-veneered fronts, sides, and tops stained dark red. There were also many with rosewood veneer—called shelf or mantel clocks.

George Washington clocks were made in France for sale in the United States for many years after the defeat of Cornwallis by the summer soldiers and sunshine patriots with the help of the French blockade.

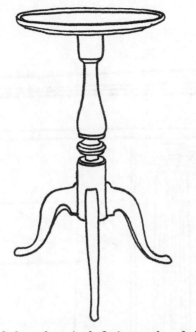

Federal candlestand of the often-indefinite style of that era. By then the posts were being turned for the fun of it, according to the turner's whim. Of course, the legs still retain a Queen Anne look because that was the most practical shape for not tripping over.

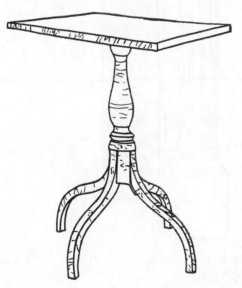

A Federal "whatzit" of a maple candlestand that combines a swelled Queen Anne post with thin tapered Hepplewhite spider legs and an oversized square-cornered top that has nothing to do with the rest of the design. Also a pointless fourth leg has been added to increase its wobble factor. A neurotic, troubled example of the elusive Federal style.

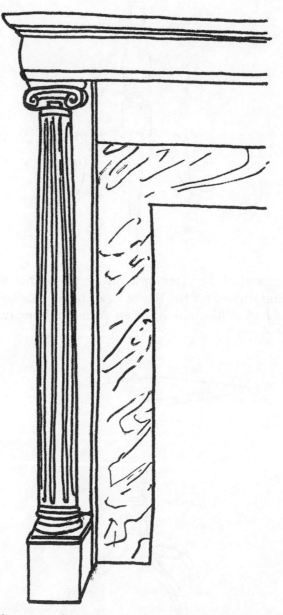

Lovely Ionic column at the side of a fireplace for a Federal house. The top is classical Empire style.

WINDSOR CHAIRS, 1720–1820

*A triumph of functionalism in design developed in America
from an English design idea*

The American Windsor chair raises a method of construction to a distinctive art form, about which many books have been written. It stands out in the history of design in the same way as does the Gothic arch and the flying buttress. And we have the same reaction to it as we do to them: "Why *not* build a chair that way? Why didn't somebody think of it a long time ago?"

To be sure, the idea of a plank seat first occurred to some unknown chairwright working around Windsor castle in England some three hundred years before the Colonial Americans picked it up in the early 1700s. But those English Windsors (see the first illustration) were thought of as garden chairs and were roughly made. Additionally they were heavy and ugly when compared to the graceful lightness of the designs developed in the American colonies.

The American Windsor chair is a true invention. It is defined by a construction method whereby its legs, arms, and back all penetrate a single thick board that is the seat.

This may sound like a pretty obvious idea except that all the chairs that came before it—and many after it—are of frame construction. In other words, they are made by fitting the legs and back into the corners of a frame on which the seat rests.

In the American Windsors the legs come right through the tops of the seats, where wooden wedges were then driven down into them for an incredible tight fit as the plank seats of pine continued to shrink over the years. The spindles and legs were made of maple and the hoops of the backs of steamed hickory.

Although Windsor chairs were most popular from 1720 to 1820, they are still being made today.

An accurate reproduction of the kind of chair that was first made around Windsor Castle in the 1500s. All known originals are in museums in England, but the style has been reproduced there since the Victorian era —the same way we Americans continue to reproduce our Windsors.

An excellent example of an American bow-back Windsor with continuous arms. Good bold leg and arm turnings and rare swelled spindles in the back. Ball-turned bottoms of the spindles "pop" into small-mouthed holes in the seat. Tops of spindles penetrate the hoop and are wedged tight.

Windsor writing chair with a fan back and braces to support the table. Not unusual, but the most valuable of all Windsor chairs. Usually found with traces of the original paint—red, black, blue, green, or mustard. Stripping of such paint is considered a sin by serious collectors.

Each of the many variations of Windsor chairs has its own descriptive name. This is called "a continuous arm bow-back rocking chair with attached fan." Not a standard model. The heavy "bamboo" turning of the legs and arms date it as a late model to boot. It probably dates from around the middle 1800s.

Fan-back Windsor with scroll-carved ears. The comparatively thin seat was popular from Pennsylvania down to Virginia, though the majority of Windsor chairs come from the New England states.

Primitive bow-back Windsor with simple turning of the legs—just about all Windsor chairs were made by country cabinetmakers. Their contemporary city cabinetmakers were turning out Chippendale for the English governing class.

While the top of this Windsor is a bow, it is called a hoop-back chair because the arms are on the end of a hoop that goes all around the back— with the spindles going through holes in the hoop. It also has knuckle carving on the ends of the arms. Made of pine, maple, and hickory in the late 1700s.

This variation would have to be called a "fan-back Windsor rocker with hooped fan and attached arms." The rockers slotted into the feet of these chairs were so thin that they were called "carpet cutters." When rockers are attached to the flattened outside of the feet, they are usually a conversion made by your great-grandfather.

A braced-back continuous arm Windsor of the finest kind and as strong today as it was two hundred years ago due to the combination of the design, the materials used, and the craftsmanship that went into it. Accurate reproductions of these chairs are still being made and, with artificial wear and distressing, are difficult to tell from the originals.

A totally American development was the practical writing-arm Windsor, possibly invented by Benjamin Franklin, who also brought us the Franklin stove and many other inventions. The drawer under the writing arm makes this one very special. Maple turnings, chestnut bending, and pine seat for bulk.

This bird-cage Windsor is definitely in the Sheraton style, which results in one of the best chair designs of all time as country cabinetmakers imitated the style popular in the cities during the Federal era.

Windsor side chair in the rod-back or bird-cage style with bamboo turn-ings. These were inspired by contact with the Orient through the clipper ships on the China Trade. But the style is still Sheraton-Windsor.

Carpet cutter with a severe rod-back or stick-back. The arms are set back to accommodate the hoop skirts of the early 1800s. Pine seat, maple legs and arms, hickory rods. All such country chairs usually found painted barn-red, blue, or mustard.

Although it was a perfectly obvious thing to do with the Windsor chair, these settees are very rare. This one is three and a half feet in length and was made circa 1800. Very expensive—worth about five times as much as a good armed Windsor.

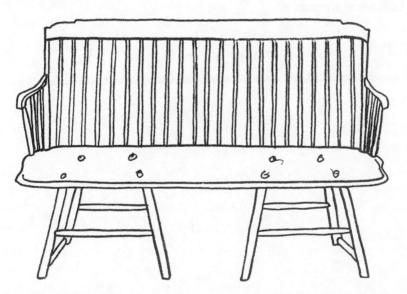

Another kind of Windsor settee was made by using the leg structures of two chairs—with the tops of legs coming right up through the seat and split with wedges to make them supertight. The result is certainly an awkward and ugly design, but for a lot of people that spells "charm," "interesting" or "quaint." *Chacun à son goût.*

Another great American invention based on the Windsor chair design was the mammy rocker. It is basically a bench with rockers. The invention is the removable fence that sticks firmly into two holes in the seat. The fence, of course, supported a blanket-wrapped baby that got rocked when Mammy rocked.

Country-made Windsor side chair with bamboo turnings. Even unpretentious chairs such as this one have great strength due to the basic Windsor design and have outlasted many of the "city-chairs" of the Federal-Sheraton period.

Around 1850 wide, flat spindles came into use, and such chairs are now called arrow-backs; this would be fine if you had no idea of what an arrow looks like. But they are strong and sturdy for use in kitchens then and now.

Arrow-back armchair from the second half of the 1800s, made of pine and maple. The rockers were added later, as was often done by the amateur furniture doctors of the time.

"Fancy chairs" were all the rage in the late 1800s as peddlers carried them out to every farmhouse in their horse-drawn wagons. They were a factory-produced version of the Windsor-Sheraton design with great hand-painted (in the factory) designs. Base paint was green or mustard.

Black was the base color by the time these Boston rockers became popular in the middle 1800s, and the decoration was many colors of bronze powder stenciled on the backs. Usually there were cornucopias with fruit spilling out to represent the happiness of a family that eats a lot of fruit.

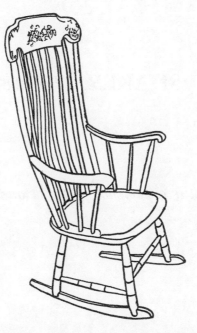

To tell the difference between a Boston rocking chair and a Salem rocking chair, like this one, requires pretty specialized knowledge and seems to be mostly in the eye of the beholder—especially since they weren't even made in Boston and Salem, but in Pennsylvania and Connecticut by the time they went into factory production.

SHAKER, 1780–1870

The ultimate experience of functionalism in design

The concept of functionalism in design is that if an object is designed solely to do the best job it is supposed to do, it will inevitably turn out to be beautiful.

This idea was first brought to public attention by artists of the Bauhaus School in Germany in the 1930s and '40s. And the principle is still widely accepted and used by designers of physical objects, from large buildings to electric shavers.

But without realizing what they were doing from an artistic point of view, a religious sect called the Shakers fully explored the idea in the furniture they created during the first half of the nineteenth century.

The Shakers withdrew from the evils of society to a number of colonies supported by farming and workshops in which they made furniture not only for themselves but also for sale to the public. They promoted the concept of functionalism because keeping with their Puritan religious beliefs—the sect died out due to their celibacy—the furniture they made wouldn't pass inspection by the elders unless it was made as "simply as possible and without ornament."

Of course since all Shakers had grown up in the real world before they joined the sect, they still had in the backs of their minds what Sheraton chairs and Queen Anne legs on candlestands looked like. But aside from that, they created a totally new, ultimately simple style of their own that is becoming ever more popular with the passing years.

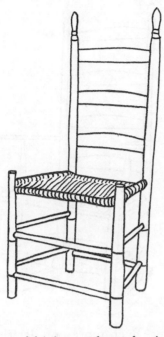

Usually made of maple and hickory, the only significant design detail of these ladder-back chairs, sold to the public by the Shakers, is the elongated bulb turnings at the top of the back posts.

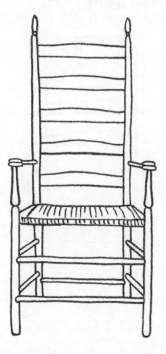

Seats were made of splint, and the ends of the slats' rungs were fastened with wooden pegs. At the ends of the arms, the "cookie" handgrips fitted to the tops of the posts were not used for decoration, but because such construction worked well and rested your hands.

Shaker rocking chairs were even more popular than their straight ones. The short arms on some were to accommodate hooped skirts. Careful fitting and well-cured wood made these chairs remarkably strong. Some are still being rocked in 150 years later.

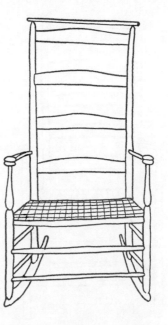

The towel bar across the top is typical of Shaker inventiveness. This chair is known as a "number seven," after the number of the factory that made it in New York State. Other colonies spread from southern New England and Pennsylvania to Ohio.

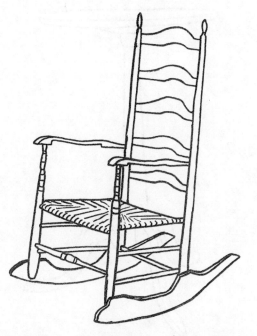

All the extra curves lead the experts to say this is not an authentic Shaker rocker, but one made by a local craftsman who didn't think Shaker rockers were fancy enough. The onion finials, however, look very Shaker. Applied rockers such as these were so thin they were called "carpetcutters."

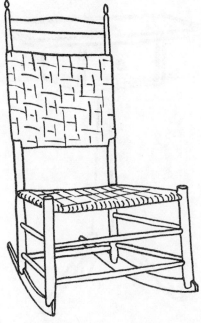

In Ohio woven fabric strips were often used instead of splint. These would likely be replacements in chairs of this kind that you would come across today.

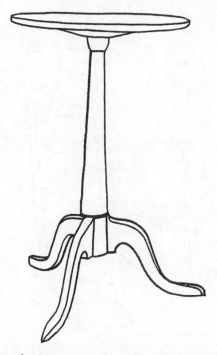

Cherry, maple, and hard pine were the woods most often used for these Shaker candlestands. With straight posts and round tops they are as simple as you can get. Not to accept that the curved leg that goes back to Queen Anne was functional would have been perverse.

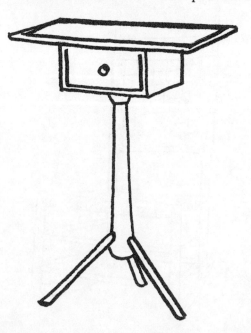

But some Shaker elders were just that perverse and insisted that those curved legs were the work of the Devil—thus this funny-looking design. But maybe you could get used to it.

Shaker work table of maple and pine. It was primarily used for sewing, but also for any other household jobs. Pieces like this were for the Shakers' own use, so they are rare compared to the chairs the Shakers sold to the public. (At their peak there were only about six thousand of the Brethren.)

Bookkeeper or accountant's desk, usually made of walnut or cherry fastened with hard maple pegs.

Shaker dry sink of pine is an almost perfect example of the purposeful use of functionalism in design. These were used for washing dishes (and small pieces of clothing) in a bowl or tin pan placed in the top.

We can only wonder what Chippendale would have thought of the strict simplicity of this high chest of drawers built by the Shakers in about 1850. Well-cured hard pine was the Shaker choice for large pieces.

This two-drawer blanket chest with a lift top is a fairly ubiquitous piece because every bedroom had one. These chests were made of pine but simply shellacked and waxed. The finish was added not because of worldly desires for beauty, but to prevent shrinkage and warping.

This four-drawer pine chest with walnut knobs is typically Shaker, but in this one the visual excitement usually associated with the functionalism just didn't come off.

Counting house desk with gallery around top to keep papers from slip-
ping off—the papers were kept in the five graduated drawers, of course.
From the early 1800s, all sealed pine.

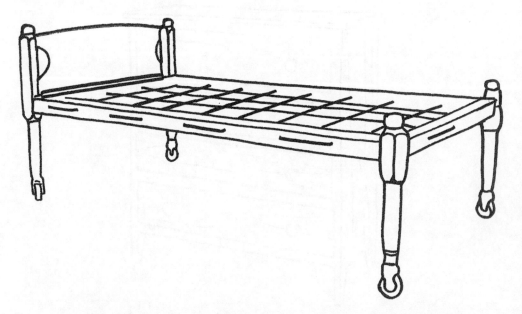

Typical of Shaker inventiveness are hard maple wheels fitted into feet of
legs of this low four-poster. Purpose was so that bed could be moved for
cleaning under it—*every* day. Shakers were scrupulously clean.

This open kitchen cupboard held dishes, silverware, and whatever linens were used on special occasions. Made entirely of sealed pine and fastened together with maple pins.

Victorian Styles

The American furniture of the industrial revolution

If the word "eclectic" wasn't invented to describe the furniture styles of the Victorian era, it should have been, for its dictionary definition is "that which is borrowed from many sources." And borrow is what our forefathers of the Victorian era did with a vengeance.

It was a time when the best of possible worlds seemed just within grasp. It was a time of expansion, travel, exploration, scientific discoveries, and the development of great industries able to mass-produce the goods that would make every man at least a prince—with a chicken in every pot—until World War I blew all that away.

But while their era lasted, the Victorians had a great appetite for life, and they were becoming familiar with all the ideas that they could borrow from the rest of the world: Gothic arches, the Italian Renaissance, the court of Louis XV, the Baroque, even the right angle—the Victorians rediscovered them all.

And they also had new hard-toothed circular saws that made it easy for them to cut oak, and carving machines that could turn out twenty ornate piano legs at a time.

Even though every furniture factory owner was his own designer and felt free to combine any styles that he thought might help his furniture sell better, some basic styles can be seen to have come into and out of fashion.

Roughly speaking the styles of the first half of the century were inspired by French styles, and the second half by English styles.

VICTORIAN EMPIRE, 1810–50

*Mahogany veneer on blocks of pine cut into wide curves
by a bandsaw*

The earliest style of Victorian furniture was a typically Americanized version of Napoleon's Empire style. It was said to be Americanized because it was simplified for purposes of mass production by means of the newly invented bandsaw that could quickly cut the style's characteristic wide curves.

Nor did this American version of Empire use the expensive Honduras mahogany and rosewood (with satinwood inlays to boot) that the French had used forty years earlier just before the French Revolution, or that the English used for their Regency style, which was a sincere imitation of Empire.

Far from it, the American-Victorian version of Empire was made of bulky blocks of New England pine. This was cut by a band saw in the wide curves the machine was capable of making and then was covered with thin sheets of inexpensive mahogany. It was a machine-made product that used low-cost materials. The industrial revolution that would provide furniture for the masses had begun.

These mahogany side chairs with veneered backs are a perfect example of America's version of the French Empire style in the first half of the 1800s. Consistently simple curves earned this furniture the nickname "Bandsaw Empire," but it is still a design that has a simple, stately dignity about it—exactly what Napoleon had in mind when he decreed the original French version.

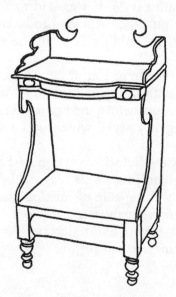

An open commode that was originally used in the bedroom circa 1830 to hold a pitcher of water, wash basin, and "thunder pot." Drawers on the sides and bottom were for combs, soap, towels, etc. The fronts of drawers and backs were faced with fancy mahogany veneers. The rest were often walnut-stained to look like red mahogany.

A perfect example of American Bandsaw Empire, this table is made entirely of bulky blocks of pine covered with figured Honduras mahogany veneers. Ornaments are solid mahogany. The double top lifts to open and swivels around to make a card table.

Double door server or sideboard in the simple curves of the American Empire style of the Victorian era. Side columns of bulky pine, the rest mahogany—all covered with fine figured Honduras mahogany veneer. In all, a fine style of furniture that is still unappreciated in the northeastern part of the United States but highly valued south of the Mason-Dixon line.

The earliest Victorian versions of the French Empire style didn't have the bandsaw curves and featured the Roman look of the side columns in this chest—as in the original French style. But construction was also of fine mahogany veneers on pine blocks—including the pine drawer fronts.

A classic American Empire chest with twisted columns of solid mahogany, the rest mahogany veneers on pine.

The pineapple tops on top of the twist-turned frontal columns make this chest a very special 1820s piece. The pineapples brought home by the early whaling ships became a symbol of prosperity.

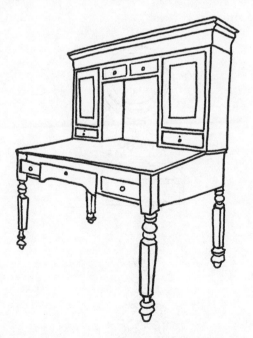

One of the famous Wells-Fargo desks found in every telegraph office along the railroad tracks in the 1800s and early 1900s. The top harks back to early squared-off Roman temple American Empire, but somehow the Eastlake influence crept into the legs, which are solid walnut. The rest is walnut, too, but with mahogany veneers.

This is called a piano desk; it has ugly legs of walnut under a top faced with mahogany veneer.

A mahogany shaving stand with an Empire-curved look about the top but an Italian Renaissance Revival bottom. Shown here because this combination of styles was so popular. The top is made of white marble.

This typical Victorian étagère demonstrates the transition from Empire to Renaissance revival, circa 1900. Ornate pieces like this were often made in rosewood.

A basically Empire-style bed that is transitional into Renaissance Revival as seen in the decoration.

VICTORIAN LOUIS XV, 1830–65

And the difference between Rococo and Baroque

Even while the Victorian Empire style was still going strong, Americans next discovered Louis XV, a style which had preceded Empire in France. And this they soon began reproducing in a range from exact reproductions to carefree digressions into exaggerated Rococo decoration, though it must be noted that the French did the same thing with the basic Louis XV style almost a century before.

There is some confusion about the use of the word "Rococo." In one sense it means the use of gentle curves found in rocks and shells. (It comes from the French words *rocailles* and *coquilles.*) And these curves found in nature were the inspiration for the style called Louis XV.

On the other hand, Rococo seems to mean to many people the flamboyant and exaggerated use of these curved forms found in nature—especially as seen in gilded leaves and vines. Basically this use of the term relates to objects made in the American Victorian era, but it is also used to describe similar flamboyant decoration of German and Italian objects.

When columns and arches from Greek and Roman architecture are added to the forms from nature in a flamboyant and exaggerated manner, the style is called *Baroque*, as in the furniture of Louis XIV.

Properly speaking, the more restrained decoration of Louis XV furniture is merely Rococo.

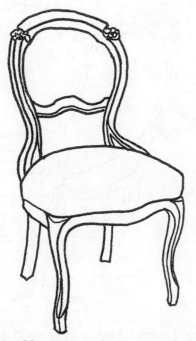

A classic side chair in the Victorian adaptation of the French style of Louis XV. A chair that is all curves in line, has hand-carved finger molding and carved grapes on the back—not attached but made out of the same block of wood.

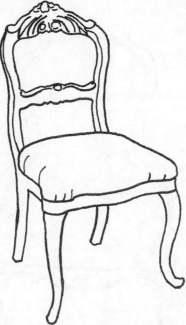

A simpler Louis XV side chair without the finger molding but with hand-carved roses and leaves on the rail. Both chairs made of solid red mahogany from Santa Domingo which by the mid-1800s was replacing Honduras as a source for this great carving wood.

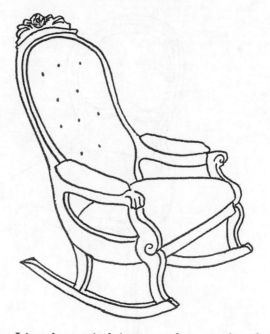

This rocker of the Lincoln period is a good example of the frequent blending of the Louis XV and Empire styles that occurred in Victorian America. The back has the finger carving and roses on the top of the rail while the front legs and arms have the familiar curves of American band-saw Empire.

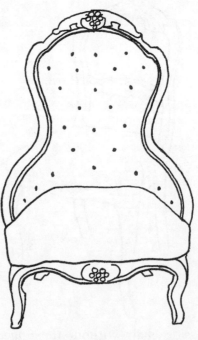

A lovely slipper chair for a lady's bedroom—so called because the seat is low to make it easy to put on your slippers, though this piece makes the typical French cabriole legs look stumpy.

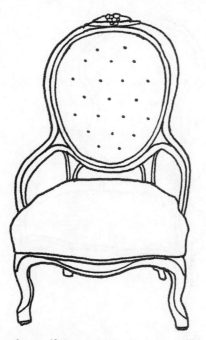

Good example of a *fauteuil* (means "open arms") armchair in the Victorian Louis XV manner. Pieces done in this style were the last of the great handmade furniture, each piece for the finger molding hand-carved and doweled together.

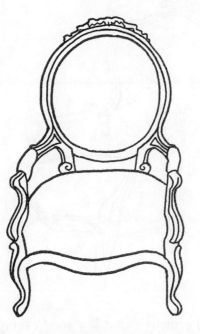

Fateuil armchair with a medallion back, which gives it a Frenchier look than the rest of these chairs. It may have been imported from France—not that unusual an occurrence.

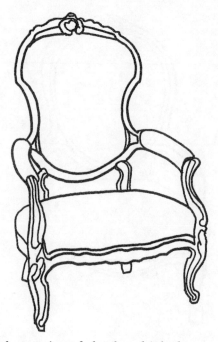

Fateuil armchair with a winged back which has a ponderous, over-important English look about it. This certainly makes it a *bad* example of the Louis XV style.

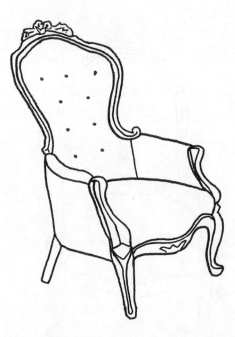

A *bergère* (closed arms) armchair that is a good example of the American Victorian Louis XV style. Hand-carved mahogany with fruit or rose carving on top. The back is called a shield or wing. Solid American black walnut, doweled together with a terrible hide-and-hoof glue.

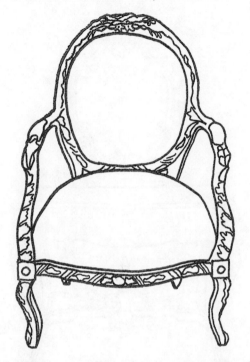

Louis XV *bergère* chair in a very French ornate manner that was just one of those many experiments they made in the Victorian era.

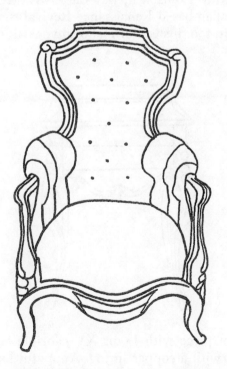

And once again an English version of the Victorian Louis XV style. The wings are *so* English—draughty castles, you know.

Charming dressing table with a tilting mirror and white marble top. The cabriol legs are surely Louis XV, but the cross stretcher is certainly moving into the Italian-based Renaissance Revival that was coming up. These are of walnut, too, instead of mahogany, as all of the Renaissance Revival would be.

A fairly nondescript piece with Louis XV cabriole legs, this is a solid walnut wine cooler with a copper lining. An awful lot of the furniture made in this period was far from pure in design. The Victorians were great experimenters.

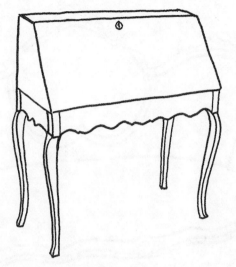

Now this is a ringer. It may look like a very restrained Victorian Louis XV piece, but it is actually a piece of golden oak made in Grand Rapids in 1910. It's a lady's desk, of course—or, as the French would say, a *bureau de dame.*

These are called medallion-back sofas. They were made of hand-carved and doweled mahogany, and once broken they are a cabinetmaker's nightmare. And they usually are broken because of the awful hide glue used to stick them together. That glue wasn't waterproof, so it moistens and gives in moist weather—which was all right for the first fifty years, but by now all these pieces are over a hundred years old.

Moving toward the Baroque style that John Belter made famous, we have this excellent piece of hand-carved mahogany with grapes and everything. A really fine example of Louis XV.

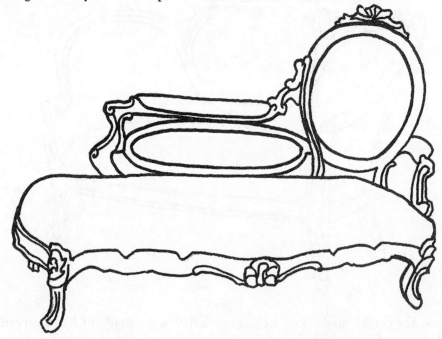

This was recently auctioned as an excellent piece of "Rococo Revival." It is a daybed and is included here because Rococo is just what the Louis XV style is. Don't let those interior decorators fool you with their fancy new names for things.

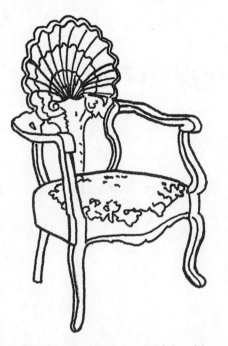

From the preceding drawings you get no idea of how eclectic the Victorian taste was during the mid-1800s, when Louis XV was the basic Victorian style. Well, here's an example of how eclectic it could get.

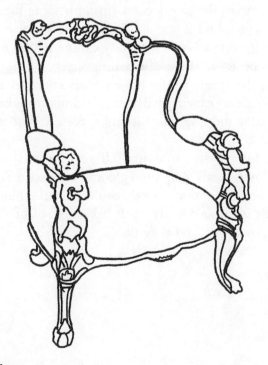

And here's another one.

BAROQUE/BELTER, 1845–65

American Baroque in laminated rosewood sheets

"Baroque" is an Italian word for an exaggerated and wildly overdecorated style of church architecture that originated in Italy around 1100.

Let's turn now to the U.S.A., circa 1850. Using this style as a model, a few sincere Victorian designers came up with some nice furniture that they called Baroque. And it was modestly popular for a while.

But then along came a New York City cabinetmaker named John Belter with a terrific idea. If he glued thin sheets of rosewood together under pressure, the result would have a cross-fiber strength that would make possible intricate carving without splitting or weakening the wood.

So that's what he did. He glued it and carved it. And everybody liked it. A lot of people still do.

Incidentally, John Belter took himself very seriously. Just before he died, he went down to his shop on a gloomy afternoon and destroyed all his patterns and molds so that nobody could ever use them again after his death. He didn't want any badly executed pieces of his invention hanging around in posterity. And they don't.

Now one more time about the words "Rococo" and "Baroque." Rococo means decorated with rocks and shells as in the gentle sparse decoration on Louis XV furniture. Baroque means decoration that is wild and flowery, exaggerated and rambunctious—as in this mirror, which happens to be of gilded brass but could also be of gilded *gesso*—plaster—used to smooth the surface of a wood carving.

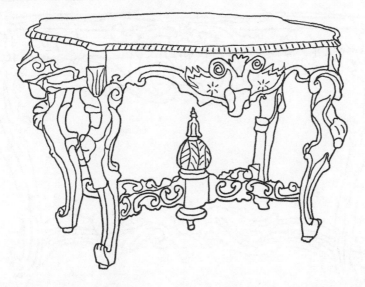

This is a Victorian-era Baroque consul table with a cross-stretcher. It is made of wood, surfaced with *gesso*, and gold-leafed—then glazed and dusted as the French would have done. It is very flowery and Baroque. It could also be in stained and varnished walnut.

A cross-stretchered wall table in the flowery Baroque style. The American Victorian pieces in this style were made of walnut or mahogany. The gilded ones found here were made in France. Real Americans don't go around gold-leafing their furniture, except maybe a mirror or two.

A rosewood center table in the florid Baroque manner that can definitely be identified as American Victorian because of its heaviness. The French version of this style was always lighter and more graceful.

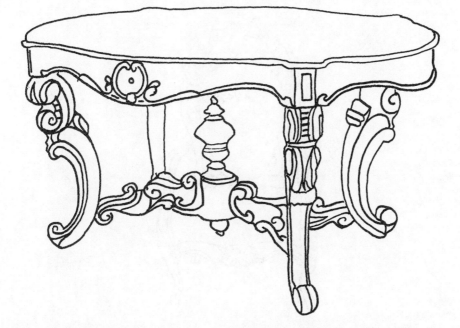

A Baroque center table of brown mahogany with a brown marble top
once owned by Jay Gould. The decoration at the center of the cross-
brace begins to look like the Italian Renaissance Revival to follow.

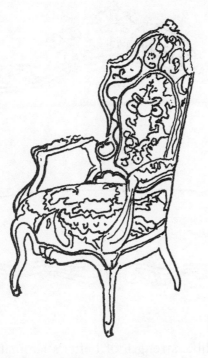

Behold Belter! A Baroque armchair made with sheets of rosewood laminated with resin in a hot press. With this super plywood Belter could
execute fine lacy carving of great strength.

Belter's rosewood chairs in the Baroque style were all made in New York City in the 1860s and now bring astronomical sums because they are unique. In this case astronomical means well over $20,000 at the time of this writing.

Because of the incredible strength of Belter's laminated rosewood, even designs like this sofa or settee are still strong and firm. If made of mahogany or walnut, a design like this would long ago have been in pieces and could never be repaired.

A Baroque chair in plain mahogany with some pierced carving but not a Belter. It's also stumpy. Not all Baroque furniture is good.

This exceptionally graceful Belter settee has grapes among the rosewood. Some Baroque furniture is magnificent.

Wonderful Belter daybed with more grapes among the pierced laminated rosewood.

An excellent solid walnut sofa with three-medallion back and eight legs —which is what you need if you don't have Mr. Belter's super strong laminated rosewood.

A real Belter that is considered his masterpiece.

GOTHIC, 1840–70

A way of expressing an inferiority complex

The Gothic style of Victorian furniture is instantly recognizable by its invariable use of the pointed Gothic arch. It became popular in the mid 1850s as a byproduct of the Gothic architecture that was sweeping the country—not for cathedrals made out of stone but for small houses made out of wood and then painted brown.

It was an odd conceit, perhaps, that houses and furniture should look like Chartres and Notre Dame, but Victorians had terrible inferiority complexes about the superiority of European art, and Gothic furniture gave them a way to express themselves.

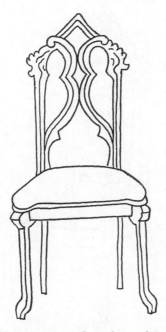

Even though it doesn't have pointed arches, this solid walnut side chair does manage to look like the inside of a cathedral. It does have a pointed top and a soaring effect created by the panels in the back. That the front legs look like Eastlake is nothing unusual for the eclectic mid 1800s.

Here the idea of the pointed Gothic arch of the great European cathedrals which Victorian tourists had discovered is combined with a more familiar Chippendale leg.

Or you can find a tall-backed churchy-looking chair like this with Renaissance Revival legs. This is still very Gothic, even if the pointed arch is missing. The whole back points up to God like a cathedral vault.

A desk like this will be seven feet long, but these pieces were built to fit in Gothic-style mansions. Always made of solid walnut with the carving glued on ("applied decoration"). Can't you just see miniature nuns walking through the arcade of cubbyholes on the top?

The elements of Gothic in this piece are its tallness and the fretwork on the glass doors—all in walnut, of course. The finials and doors relate to the Renaissance Revival, which was popular at the same time.

If this bed doesn't look just like the cathedral at Chartres, I've never seen a picture of it.

Even John Henry Belter got into the Gothic act, but the best he could do was to put massive feet on this basically Empire sleigh bed with his pierced laminated rosewood carvings in the Baroque manner. Oh, those eclectic Victorians!

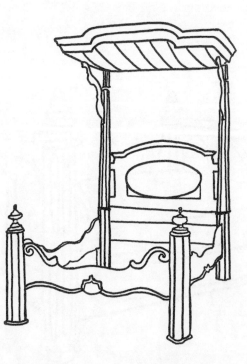

The footposts of this bed are the Gothic element of it. The back and top are Empire/Eastlake. Sometimes the eclectic Victorians just went too far!

The top and drawers of this secretary desk are American Empire, the legs heading toward Eastlake, and the glass doors have Gothic pointed arches. Victorian.

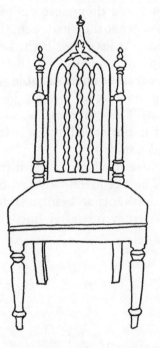

The pointed back of this upholstered side chair is a good example of ecclesiastic-looking Gothic—with Renaissance Revival front legs.

RENAISSANCE REVIVAL, 1850–85

Supposedly inspired by the architecture
of the Italian Renaissance

In the prosperous years after the Civil War, Americans toured Italy in force, and when they got home they were delighted by a style of furniture that reminded them of what they had seen: the Renaissance architecture of Florence and Rome. At least that is the best explanation anybody has been able to think up, for this most Victorian of furniture styles.

At its best it is a brown walnut chest or table with a white marble top. But mostly it is a conglomerate of design ideas that the Victorians thought looked European. The emphasis was definitely on decoration rather than design. So it is not a real style. It is fussy. It is what gives Victorian furniture a bad name.

However, we all recognize it when we see it in movies about the wild West and railroad barons and crooked bankers. So there is a sort of historical romance about it. Rather than being a style, it is the furniture of a particular period in our history just after our Civil War.

Coming along in the late 1800s, Renaissance Revival was the first furniture made in the new furniture factories that were starting up all over the country—especially in Grand Rapids, Michigan, near the great walnut forests. And this chair is as close to the design idea as can be found. It just *looks* Italian, as it was intended to.

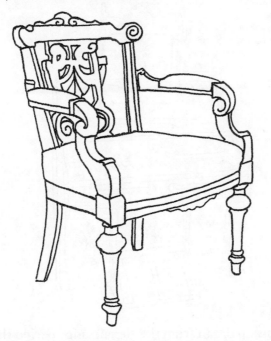

But just as Renaissance is this chair with its trumpet legs from the William and Mary period and the broad Empire curves of the front arms and Eastlake rail on the back.

The overdecoration on the top of the headboard is typical of Renaissance furniture. The columns at the sides of the footboard look Gothic, but then the two styles are cousins with roots in the same cathedrals that the Victorian tourists had become familiar with.

An all-walnut pump organ from the Renaissance period that was made in Grand Rapids and sold through a mail-order catalogue like Sears, Roebuck & Co. In the late 1800s everybody made Renaissance, and they made it anyway they wanted to.

On the other hand, many Renaissance pieces have the florid, Baroque look of this hall piece with mirror and white marble tops to the shelves and base. The wood is walnut with some rosewood-veneer panels. Another of the many faces of the Renaissance Revival.

Can a Roman temple with gilded caryatids be Renaissance Revival? You bet your life it can if a railroad baron will pay for it. Made of walnut, of course, it is a china cabinet or display case.

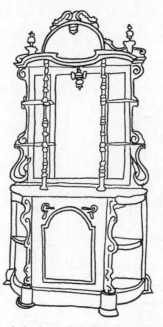

Parlor pieces with a lot of shelves for displaying small objects were called *étagères* and were very popular in the late 1800s. Once again we have the florid, Baroque look that kept breaking out in the Renaissance period. Not a style, a *period*.

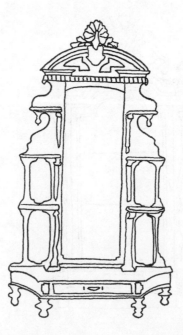

A combination hall mirror and *étagère* for displaying small vases and statuettes of ladies in veils. Made in a Midwest furniture factory to look European.

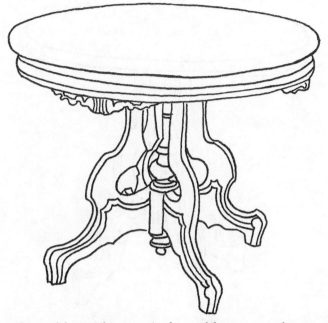

A walnut parlor table with a typical marble top resting on the oddly shaped legs that were popular in the period we call Renaissance Revival. This type of leg was used in the cathedral furniture of the Middle Ages and is basically Baroque in the sense of being exaggerated curves of a pointless pretentious kind. Just right.

Of course this is a French table in the manner of Louis XV with cabriol legs squared up in the Empire manner. But it has a white marble top, and it definitely falls into the conglomerate we call Renaissance Revival.

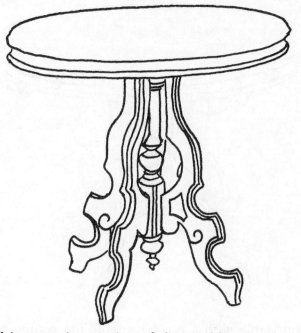

A small and inexpensive version of the marble-topped parlor table, the base of this one is actually made of inexpensive pine stained to look like walnut. A big seller throughout the Midwest.

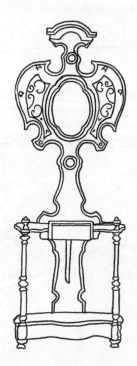

In the Victorian era people needed a lot more hall pieces than we do now. This one was a walnut mirror and umbrella stand with pegs for hanging coats. Grotesque? No, just Baroque in the curves of the top.

This *étagère* looks like Biedermeier to me—a German version of Empire. Things like this just happened when the plant manager was in charge of design in a Victorian furniture factory.

Ah, such restraint in the middle of the Renaissance Revival. Made of walnut, with glass doors, it is a bookcase-desk or secretary.

EASTLAKE, 1870–90

The moral triumph of the straight line over degenerate curves

A certain geometric look in ornamentation is the tell-tale detail of this stuffy, undistinguished style that for some reason has always appealed to otherwise reasonable Midwesterners.

The style was invented by an English reformer—named Eastlake, of course—who was wild about straight lines and hated curves. Ridiculous? Eastlake once wrote in a book intended to reform all Americans: "The tendency of the present age runs exclusively to curves. A curve in the back of a sofa is manifestly inconvenient, for it is either too high in one place or too low in another. Chairs are curved to ensure the greatest amount of ugliness and the least amount of comfort. The legs of cabinets are curved in a senseless manner and become weak. Tables are curved in every direction and are inconvenient to sit at."

So much for Louis XV and his chairs that look poised to jump in the air.

The Eastlake idea that straight lines and honest factory construction were better than curves and hand-carving is well illustrated by this combination chest of drawers and commode. It is made of walnut, and even the bailles on the drawer pulls are square.

The squareness of Eastlake is also seen in this oak dresser with its serviceable white marble top, upon which was placed a china bowl and pitcher used for washing.

Eastlake drawers invariably had straight lines across them inscribed in the wood. The basic tool for making Eastlake was obviously a table saw. This piece is "late" Eastlake because it is made of oak instead of walnut. With white marble top and bevel-edge, heavy plate-glass mirror.

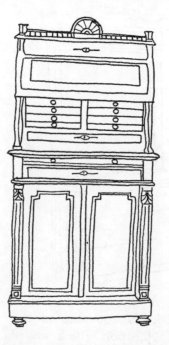

Good Eastlake dental cabinet of walnut with a lot of burl walnut veneer.

But Victorians couldn't resist fooling around with styles—as in this dresser with an Eastlake top on an Empire-looking chest of drawers with a white marble top.

An Eastlake secretary desk that is an original design as so many Victorian pieces were.

The trouble with sticking to the Eastlake principle that straight lines are better than curves became apparent when it came to the chairs. This one is pretty straight, even in the wonderful braces from back to seat, which are a very Eastlake feature—making these chairs *very* strong. But the turned front legs—from Sheraton—could have been square like the back legs.

But curves were hard to repress, and they quickly took over in the back rails, seat braces, and the shape of the seat. Walnut with walnut burl veneer on the back.

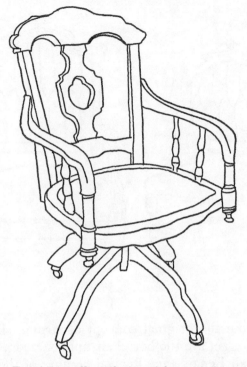

Here a very popular Eastlake office chair with a minimum of curves and a heavy spring under the seat so you could lean back in it as you swiveled around and rolled on the brass coaster. Walnut.

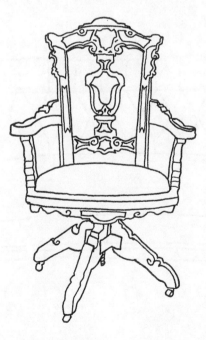

Tilt-back Eastlake office chair made in a factory used to making Renaissance Revival furniture—which is a hard habit to break.

The farthest from the original concept of strong, simple, straight-line furniture that we get are the horsehair-upholstered parlor sets that look downright Italian Renaissance Revival because of the decoration—even if only the rail curves. Louis XVI legs, indeed!

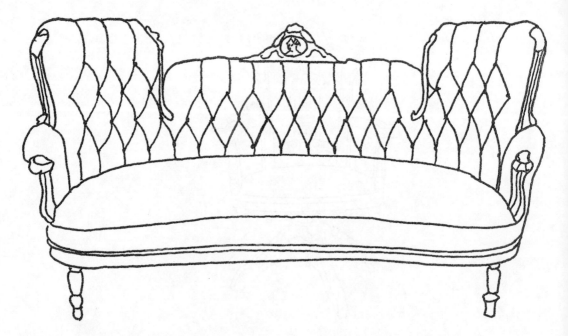

Upholstered settee from a parlor set sold at the time as Eastlake. Those people just couldn't keep the French and Italian curves from creeping back in.

The furniture factories that had been making tables in the curve-oriented Renaissance Revival style, based on old Italian architecture, did their best to make them look like the new Eastlake style. The best they could do was make the top rectangular and run those Eastlake lines up and down the front of the legs. Now this is a real Victorian parlor table.

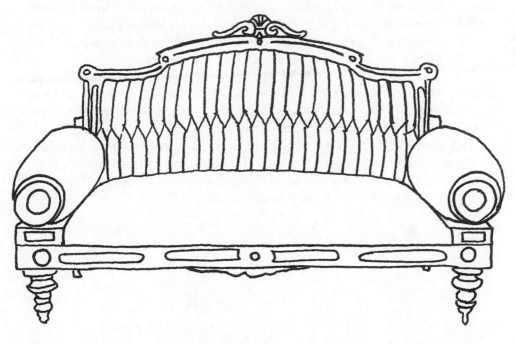

Would you believe, an Eastlake couch with a Turkish influence in the ottoman-like arms? Well, that's what it is.

GOLDEN OAK, 1890–1920

Not really a style—but a nice hard wood!

The term "Golden Oak" has been widely abused, because there is no such style at all. The trouble is that whatever style of furniture you make out of oak, it is hard to notice anything except the wood. But when it came into use in the early 1900s, it was used to make furniture in many styles. Some of these—such as Empire and Louis XV—had been popular in the preceding Victorian years. There were two new ones—Mission and Eastlake—and a lot of office furniture.

The best of the pieces made of oak at this time were the pressed-back chairs, which were designed to be made of oak and turned out to be a visual success. They are a shining example of functionalism in design working out the way it is supposed to.

And there is a certain grotesque charm to the grossly overcarved ice-boxes and buffets whose lion's heads and paws are reminiscent of Chippendale—or maybe of a nightmare Chippendale had. Perhaps "Carnival Chippendale" would be the best term for them.

The top of the line in Golden Oak is this ornately carved ice box of circa 1890 to 1910 and others like it. The ice went in the top, the food in the bottom door, and the melting ice drained out the bottom into a pan. Carvings were glued on.

"Ubiquitous" is the word for these gingerbread clocks with good Victorian brassworks and glass doors mounted in pressed oak panels—pressed with steel dies under enormous pressure to imitate carving. Almost every house had one.

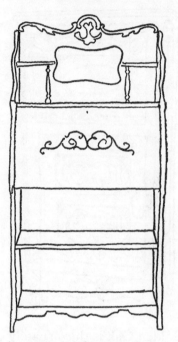

Possibly the most favorite piece of Golden Oak is this shallow up-against-the-wall desk with a beveled glass mirror at the top and carvings glued on the top. The front falls forward to reveal small drawers and cubby-holes. It only stands out from the wall a foot when closed.

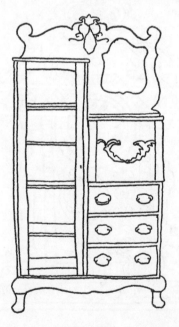

Really superb in super-hard Golden Oak with a little Art Nouveau on the top is this combination bookcase (with glass door), fall front desk, and set of drawers that is only eighteen inches deep. And the mirror is bevel-edged to match the eccentric shape of its frame.

Also ubiquitous to the era were these round-topped oak dining tables with a wide variety of pedestal styles. This style is undoubtedly called Roman Empire. By now most of these have had the tops of their pedestals sawed off to lower the tops to cocktail-table height.

For some reason all square Golden Oak dining tables are so ugly they are funny. The center leg of this one is used to support four extra leaves when the ends are pulled apart. And even when closed it is too big to make a cocktail table out of it.

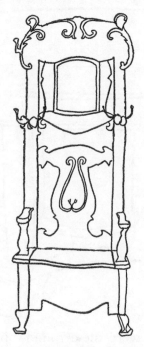

Golden Oak hall piece with brass hooks for hanging clothes, a mirror for adjusting your hat, and a box in the seat for storing your galoshes. And you could sit in it, too.

Desks that closed with roll tops or cylinders to conceal the clutter were all the rage in the Victorian office. In a hundred styles, they were made of walnut as well as oak.

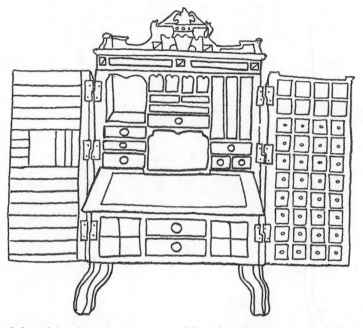

Designed for shipping magnates and heads of great corporations, several thousand of these desks were made by the factory of Charles Wooton, who even had his design patented. The writing surface slides in, and the many-drawered sides fold in and close like a book.

Any resemblance to the Baroque furniture of Louis XIV is fully intended in this grandiose partner's desk with its solid carved legs. It's a historical monument to the enthusiasm and exuberance of the American people of the booming Victorian era.

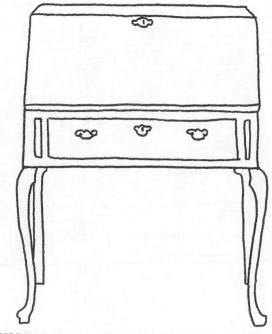

Very Louis XV-looking—and on purpose—is this slant-front desk of
shining Golden Oak, circa 1915.

Massive, dominating sideboards of Golden Oak were the dining room
battleships of the period. Like the dinosaurs, their sheer size was the
cause of their gradual extinction; the only call for them now is to decorate Victorian bars, and how many of them have you seen lately?

Would you believe our exuberant Victorian ancestors even imposed the American Bandsaw Empire style on Golden Oak as evidenced in this desk. Or was it vice versa?

A Golden Oak dresser with soft curves and a graceful simplicity that is in great contrast to the flamboyant iceboxes of only ten years before.

A classic "pressed-back" Golden Oak side or table chair. The many millions manufactured are all still as strong as the day they were made because of the hardness of the oak used. It is so dense and hard that it contracts and expands with heat and moisture very little more than cast iron does. Also important are the braces from seat to back. The ultimate combination of design and material—a chair of functional beauty that may last forever.

Victorians were fascinated by experimentation and variations. So the basic graceful side chair of the period could quickly degenerate into a fat ugly rocker like this pressed-back one.

MISSION, 1895–1915

*A misnamed expression of the wholesome ideal
in American life*

If it looks like the crate your furniture came in—that's Mission. Well, almost. For Mission was made of solid-oak boards stained dark brown and fastened together with such soundness that the only way you can break Mission is to run over it with a tank.

Around the turn of the century, it expressed the "Teddy" Roosevelt ideal of a wholesome return to simplicity, physical strength, and spiritual integrity.

The first of it was designed and made by an entrepreneur named Gustav Stickley in Binghamton, N.Y., and pieces with his "Stickley" or "Craftsman" label on them are incredibly valuable today. But many imitators sprang up, and the style was even widely sold by Sears, Roebuck and Company.

The name Mission is a confusing one. It certainly seems to suggest that the design has something to do with our Spanish Southwest along the Mexican border. But weirdly enough the name Mission was given to it by a Chicago promoter who didn't think Craftsman sounded romantic enough for his customers.

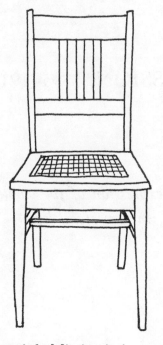

Although this chair is certainly Mission in its straight-line simplicity, the trouble with it is that sometimes pure simplicity doesn't have any flavor. But this problem is overcome in most of the pieces that follow.

A perfect example of what the Mission style was is what happened when the style was applied to a Golden Oak dining table circa 1915, when Mission was at its peak.

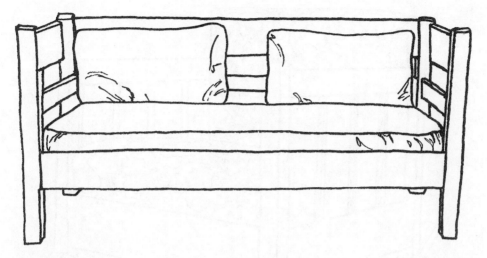

In this tale of two couches—or a couch and a settee—we here have Mission at its best . . .

. . . and Mission at its worst—when the managers of many furniture factories were their own designers.

For another example of good Mission and bad, here is the kind of Mission found in houses designed by Frank Lloyd Wright . . .

. . . as opposed to the kind of Mission sold through the Sears, Roebuck catalogues.

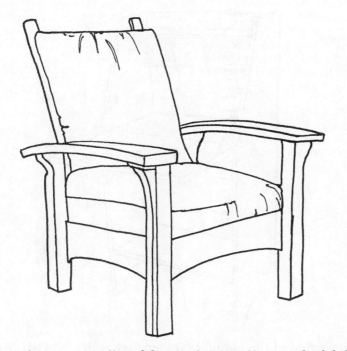

This time we have an excellent Morris chair with a wonderful Art Nouveau look in its gentle curves. How beautiful compared to . . .

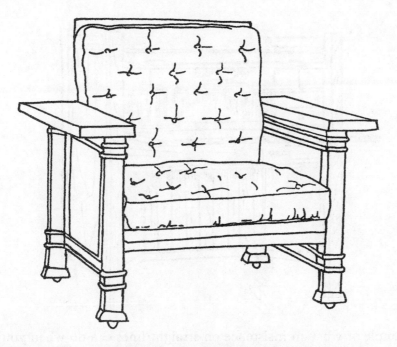

. . . this ponderous imitation of a Midwestern bank in a dusty plains town. Since this chair was actually designed by Frank Lloyd Wright, we are once again reminded that nobody is perfect.

A Mission version of the popular Golden Oak wall desks being produced at the same time. For Mission the oak was darkened with acid, a process called fuming. The resulting color was an unattractive blackish-brown, so for modern use Mission is often bleached or sanded down to a lighter color.

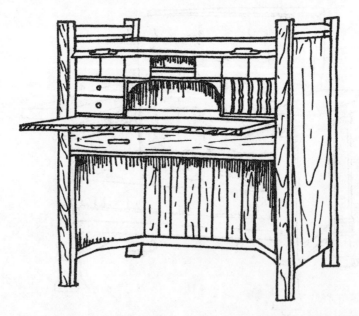

An example of what an insistence on straight lines can do when you are designing a fall front desk in the Mission style. This is the extreme opposite from the curvaceous Louis XV style that seemed about to jump into the air. But this is not Stickley Mission; it's bad factory Mission.

An office desk of Golden Oak, but obviously under the Mission influence.
It doesn't come off badly at all—just innocuous.

Here we have the same desk in true Mission style.

This dining room server is another example of the innocuous thing that happens halfway between Golden Oak and Mission.

Pure Mission and a successful design statement. But you can't help wondering what the Philadelphia Chippendale clock makers would have thought of it.

This library table is an unexplainable aberration by a very free-lance designer who wanted to improve on the Mission style.

A leather cushioned sitting stool which is another example of how a basically good design idea can be made grotesque.

ART NOUVEAU, 1895–1915

The French "grapevine" furniture

Around 1900 the French revived the idea of incorporating the curved lines of nature into the design of furniture. The first time this had resulted in the great style of Louis XV, described as "Rococo," since it used the curves of rocks *(rocailles)* and shells *(coquilles)*. But this time they went even farther and decided to use the curves of grapevines, which made some pieces look as if the wood in them was still growing.

For about twenty years this style was not only the leading one in France, but was popular all over Europe, even in England among the upper crust. So while little of it was made in this country, a lot of it has become available over the years.

The most important thing that happened in the United States during the popularity of the Art Nouveau period was the use of its flowing lines in Tiffany lamps and other glassware. But traces of it also appear in Golden Oak and other furniture being made at the time.

Although the Art Nouveau style originated in France, it reached total fulfillment in the U.S. table lamps made by Louis Comfort Tiffany. The bronze base is in the form of a tree trunk with flowing roots; the stained-glass shade represents a fruit tree in bloom.

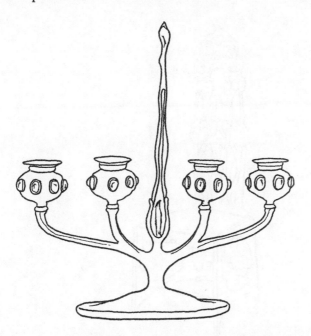

Since the idea was to follow the lines of nature, this candlestand has four candle holders with bullfrog eyes of glass that are supported by vines that flow into the base. The central stalk is topped with a rosebud reaching to the sky.

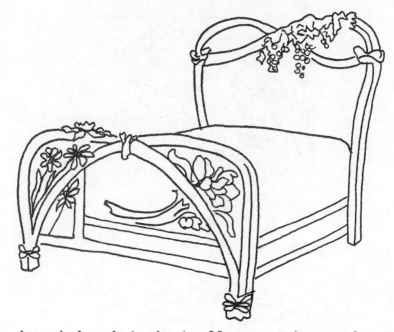

A rare brass bed made in the Art Nouveau style around 1900. The twisted "limbs" are of brass tubing; the grapes on the head and flowers on the footboard are of cast bronze. The original model of this American-made bed was a French one made of walnut and fruit wood.

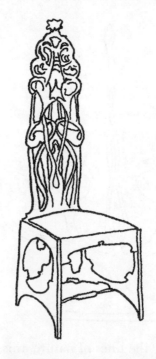

A typically American use of the French Art Nouveau style in which the carved back looks as if it were growing in a swamp while the seat and base seem to come from Morocco.

A typically free-wheeling Victorian chair with the look of Art Nouveau in its back, a round Louis XVI seat, Italian Renaissance style cabriol legs, and Chippendale claw-and-ball feet.

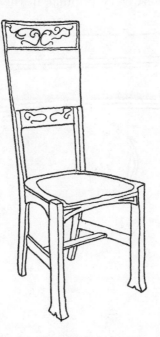

The Art Nouveau style didn't always have to hit you on the head. In this side chair of oak made around 1900, the "lines of nature" are gently suggested in the feet of the front legs, the braces under the seat, and the floral decorative carving.

Usually made out of steamed birch, bentwood furniture was easily adapted to the Art Nouveau style—as in this washstand with tilting mirror, also called a shaving stand. The wood was stained to resemble mahogany. Such pieces were very popular in the early 1900s.

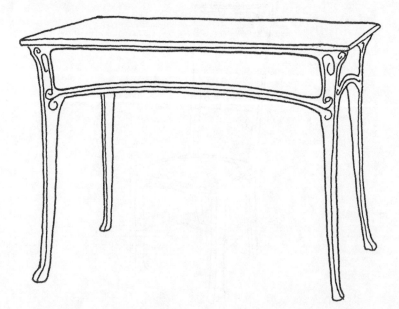

The Art Nouveau style reached magnificence in the delicate but strong lines of this library table. Although the legs are long curves outward instead of cabriole, the resemblance to the style of Louis XV—the other style of curves—is remarkable. French is curves, and curves are French.

Made of solid oak, this library table is a curious mixture of the French curves of Art Nouveau and the straight-lined solidity of the English variant of the Mission style that—emerged around the early 1900s.

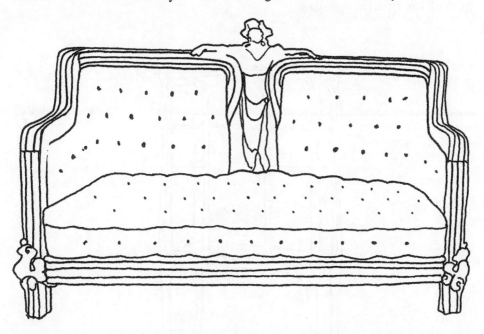

Upholstered settee made of fruit wood in the flowing lines of nature that characterise the Art Nouveau style. How it manages to end up looking heavy and cumbersome is just one of those triumphs of human incompetence. Compare with the library table two drawings back! And the "leaping" *étagère* that follows.

A popular *étagère* or piece for displaying curios and small *objéts d'art.*
Usually made of rosewood or good figured mahogany, this design has the
French "spring" of the Louis XV style in spite of the unrelated square-
ness of the central mirror.

Delightful China cabinet that once again has the look of Louis XV.

ART DECO, 1918–35

The "modern" look of the 1930s

Like Art Nouveau, Art Deco was also originally a French idea, but this one really caught on in the United States during the 1930s and '40s.

It had that "modern" look that excited people of those years. It was simplified, streamlined. It *looked* as if it was made by machinery. It looked as if it *was* machinery. It looked like what a Hollywood star would have in her bedroom—and Rita Hayworth did.

Actually Art Deco exists on two levels of quality. The pieces made in France and by a few cabinet shops in the United States were of high quality in both workmanship and in the woods and finishes used. But the great mass of Art Deco pieces were quickly and cheaply made to satisfy a great popular demand. But even these inexpensive pieces that can currently be found in flea markets have a high novelty value in interior decoration.

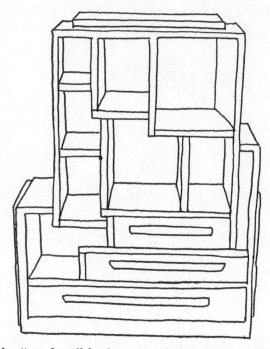

A rage for the "modern" look swept the country in the 1930s, and many furniture manufacturers turned out boxy-looking pieces like this combination of shelves and drawers that were particularly useful for furnishing small apartments because they were two pieces in one.

The stark simplicity of the Art Deco style was a boon to the manufacturers—all straight saw cuts and almost any wood sprayed with beige lacquer. Most pieces such as these shelves were first made by quality manufacturers of hardwoods covered with fine colored finishes, then quickly copied by mass producers in pine that was either unfinished or lightly stained brown and given an unrubbed coat of lacquer.

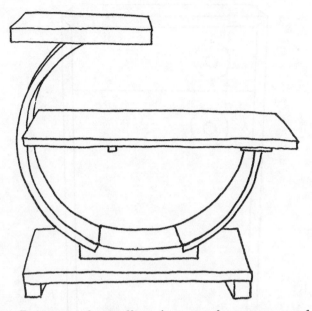

Although Art Deco was basically a boxy style, curves made of molded plywood do often appear in the highest quality pieces. These would be veneered with "blond" or bleached mahogany or thick coats of lacquer. Blonding was a process in which the mahogany was bleached and then wiped with pale yellow lacquer before some final coats of clear lacquer were applied and rubbed down.

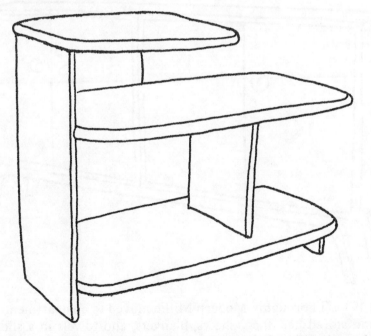

Maple wood was often used for table-top sets of shelves like these, for use next to a chair or the end of a couch. Cocktails on top and books below— sophistication, indeed!

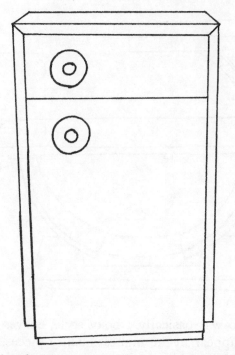

About as far as simplicity can go, this is a modern *commode* of all things, to go next to a bed. In this quality piece the hardwood core boards are covered with veneered blond mahogany.

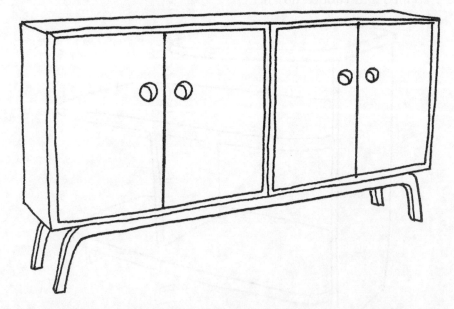

In the 1930s Thoroughly Modern Millie moved to an apartment in Memphis and stored her linen, sheets, blankets, and towels in a sliding-door cabinet like this one. Finger holes replace handles. There are two shelves inside. These cabinets come in either blond mahogany or pale beige lacquer finish.

Typical Art Deco chest of drawers with spun-brass drawer pulls was
made in furniture factories all over the country and sold through depart-
ment stores. Veneered with blond mahogany, fine hand-rubbed clear lacquer finish. It is a quality lacquer that is immune to white rings from wet
glasses, but the color sure makes cigarette burns stand out.

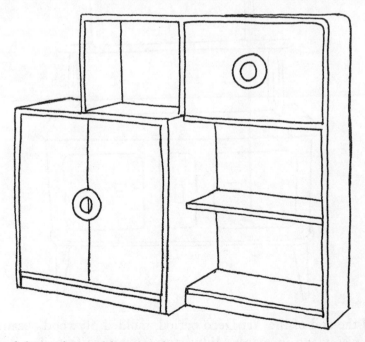

Chippendale et al. would certainly turn over in their graves if they could
see this 1930s version of a secretary, but such pieces have recently become highly desirable as the era that produced them slides gently into
history.

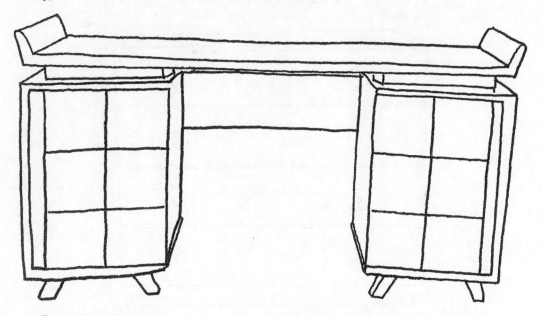

Dressing table from a bedroom set finished in black and blond lacquer. Custom-made pieces like this one are highly valued because they are probably one of a kind.

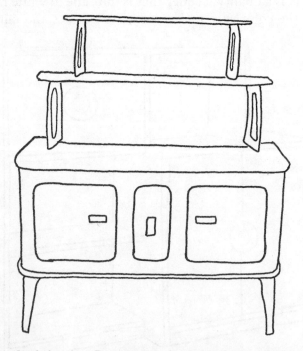

Toward the end of the Art Deco period, molded plywood became popular and was made in many Midwestern furniture factories. The wood was usually blond mahogany veneer over plywood especially designed for molding in a hot press—just as John Henry Belter once did with rosewood veneers.